THE PROPHET OF MERCY

MUHAMMAD

Scenes from His Life

By
Osman Nuri Topbaş

ERKAM PUBLICATIONS

© Erkam Publications 2001 / 1422 H

Published by:
Erkam Publications
Ikitelli Organize Sanayi Bölgesi
Turgut Özal Cd. No: 117/2
Ikitelli, Istanbul, Turkey
Tel: (90-212) 671-0700 pbx
Fax: (90-212) 671-0717
E-mail: erkam@altinoluk.com
Web site: http://www.altinoluk.com

ISBN: 975-6736-28-3

Translator	: Abdullah Penman
Editors	: Selman Slocum
	John Yasin
Cover design	: Altinoluk Graphics
Typeset by	: Altinoluk Graphics
Printed by	: Erkam Printhouse

TABLE OF CONTENTS

TRANSLATOR'S PREFACE

*W*hen I was asked to translate this book from Turkish to English, I hesitated. Nevertheless, after thoroughly reading it, I became convinced that both English speaking Muslims and non-Muslims alike would enjoy it and would benefit from it by learning an aspect of the Prophet Muhammad's life that usually has been –intentionally or unintentionally– ignored. The aspect being referred to is his mercy, which is without doubt the prevailing theme of his entire life. Today, both Muslims and non-Muslims need to know that no one other figure in history can approach the mercy exemplified in the life of the Prophet Muhammad. They also need to know that his example is especially relevant in a world that has become universally more and more dominated by selfish and materialistic life styles. This book is a call to mercy both in our social relations as well as in our interactions with our natural environment through a deep revisiting of the exemplary life of the mercy to all mankind, Prophet Muhammad.

This book is an excellent introduction to life of the Prophet Muhammad by a well-known Turkish author who has dedicated his life to learn, to practice and to spread the Prophet's teachings. The author opens a humble window for those who want to gaze into the life of a man whose example is followed today by one fifth of the world's population. No other historical figure has influenced humanity and human history more than Prophet Muhammad. He taught one of the major world religions and he laid during his lifetime the foundation of one of the brightest civilizations the world has known. However, according to this book these are not the most important features of the Prophet's life. Instead, the book demonstrates that the greatness of the Prophet Muhammad arises from the fact that he practiced the highest moral principles in his life and in his social relations. Thus, he touched the hearts of the poor, the needy and the oppressed and was able to elevate them to the level of being teachers for all of humanity. His love, his compassion and his mercy encompassed not only humans but also animals and even planets. He was a Prophet remarkable for his human face and for his love for all.

The title that was given to Prophet Muhammad by Allah in the Holy Qur'an is "the Mercy for the Worlds". The human world is just one of the worlds created by Allah, "the Lord of the Worlds." The endless and eternal compassion of Allah who named Himself as the Most Compassionate and the Most Merciful manifested itself in the life of His Messenger to humanity. This compassion never decreased in the course of conquering Arabia and defeating his enemies, to the contrary his enemies even benefited from his mercy on many occasions as history has recorded. He never hit a child, a slave or a woman and strongly prohibited such behavior and never refused to assist those who approached him in need.

Loving Prophet Muhammad is a part of the Islamic faith. As all Muslims are required to love Allah, so are they also required to love His Messenger. Without this love, faith is unacceptable. And their love for Allah and His Messenger must be above and beyond their love for anything else. Muslims display their love and respect for Prophet Muhammad by honoring him whenever his name is mentioned with the saying: Peace be upon him or in Arabic "sallallahu 'alayhi wa sallam". This is a part of their etiquette in relationship to the Prophet. As one learns about his life, this love naturally grows in one's heart and eventually fills it to entirety.

The author, Osman Nuri Topbaş currently lives in Istanbul. He has received both a traditional and a modern education. He has written many books covering different aspects of Islam as a religion and as a civilization. One recurring subject in his writings bears on demonstrating the importance of mercy, of love and of care in our social relations as the very fabric of an authentic Islamic way of life. This book, which was written in a climate of love for the Prophet Muhammad, peace be upon him, reflects his mercy, the most distinguished characteristics of the Prophet's way of life and morality. It intends to guide people to kindness and refinement of heart, and thus aims to help them gain happeness in this world and the Hereafter.

The information presented in this book has been collected from the most reliable and earliest possible scholarly sources which are thoroughly cited in footnotes. The sayings of the Prophet Muhammad have been chosen only from authentic collections of hadith. For those who desire to obtain further information the Arabic sources have been provided.

I have a strong feeling that this book will fill a gap in literature about the Prophet Muhammad by bringing to the fore a most neglected side of his life: his mercy. In a world dominated by the necessity of dialogue among civilizations and religions, it is what we need most. The call of Allah to mercy through His Messenger Muhammad must echo in the hearts of those who follow in his footsteps. No better source of mercy, than those individuals chosen by Allah to guide humanity, can be found.

Abdullah Penman

THE PRIDE OF THE UNIVERSE

MAY PEACE AND GREETINGS BE UPON HIM
(Sallallahu 'Alayhi wa Sallam)

"He indeed shall be successful who purifies himself." **(Qur'an, al-Ala, 87/14)**

Greetings to Muhammad Mustafa, mercy to the worlds of humans and jinn!

Greetings to Muhammad Mustafa, messenger to the worlds of humans and jinn!

Greetings to Muhammad Mustafa, Imam of the two holy sanctuaries in Mecca and Medina!

Greetings to Muhammad Mustafa, grandfather of Hasan and Husayn!

Allah, the Most Glorified, has embraced the world with His endless mercy. He granted the highest place in the universe to humans, who are the perfect outcome of His mercy and compassion. Allah also endowed man with attributes so as to make him qualified for such a position.

Even this distinguished position has not been enough for humans to reach truth to the extent that Allah willed. So they were endowed with such divine blessings as reason and intuition. Furthermore, another gift was added to these in the form of guidance by the messengers of Allah. Thus, the divine support extended to humans on the path to Allah has been perfectly paved. The absolute height of this divine help was the light of Muhammad, who was the last prophet in fulfilling this mission to the world, and whose physical presentation to our world as the Messenger was a gift.

How He Honored the World

The Prophet –may peace and greetings be upon him– who is the zenith of the chain of creation, came to this world on Monday, the 12th of Rabi al-Awwal, which corresponds to the 20th April of 571 CE. He was born just before sunrise.

With his emergence, divine mercy flooded into this world. The colors of morning and night changed. Feelings became deeper. Words, friendships and pleasures opened up endlessly. Everything gained a new meaning and a new pleasure. Idols were shaken and shattered. In Madayin, the land of the glorious kings of Iran, palaces and towers were destroyed. The water of lake Sava was drawn in and the whole lake dried as the muddy waters of oppression began to vanish.

Hearts were flooded by the showering of divine mercy and blessings.

His father went to Damascus for trade and on his way home he passed away in Medina, only two months before his birth.

Following Arab custom, the blessed child remained in the care of his milk mother, Halima, for four years.

At the age of six, with the purpose of visiting the grave

of her late husband, his mother Aminah took Muhammad (peace be upon him) and Umm Ayman, the maid of the family, to Medina. A terminal illness was awaiting Aminah during the trip. She passed away in a place called Abwa. The poet described it as follows:

O the deceased, sleeping in Abwa!
Blossomed in your garden
The most beautiful rose in the world…

Muhammad (peace be upon him), thus, became an orphan and returned to Mecca with Umm Ayman.

At the age of eight, he lost his grandfather, Abd al-Muttalib. Not long after, he also lost his uncle Abu Talib; who had defended him selflessly. Thus, all of his visible supporters had departed. After that, the sole protector and teacher he had was his Lord. In fact, these visible care-takers during the weakest period of his life were given to him based on the divine wisdom that he would eventually be a perfect example for the whole of humanity to follow.

His childhood and youth as an orphan were passed in chastity and the highest morality, which indicated his prospects for a bright future.

❀

When he reached the age of 25, Muhammad (peace be upon him) married Khadijah, may Allah be pleased with her. She was a noble woman from Quraysh, the ruling tribe of

Arabia. The noble Khadijah became a source of support for him as she put her life and wealth at his service. Khadijah, fifteen years older than Muhammad (peace be upon him), was a widow with children. The Prophet had a beautiful relationship with her which is exemplary for the whole world.

When he was alone in his struggle, she was the first to support him. For instance, when the first revelation came to the Prophet Muhammad (peace be upon him) in a cave on Mount Hira, he was shaken by the enormous responsibility he had been given by Allah. Immediately, he returned home.

When he came back frightened from the cave of Hira he said:

– O Khadijah! Who will believe me?

This blessed wife answered Muhammad (peace be upon him) by saying:

– By Allah! Allah will never forsake you because you care for your relatives, you shoulder the burden of those who cannot carry it themselves, you are charitable to the poor and you help them attain to what others cannot. You are generous to guests. You help people in challenges they face on the right path... O, Messenger of Allah! I will accept you and believe in you. Invite me first to the path of Allah! [1]

So she was the first to believe and she was his first supporter.

The Prophet (peace be upon him) never forgot her deep

---

(1) Bukhârî, *Zakât* 1; Muslim, *Îmân* 12; Nasâî, *Salât* 10; Ahmad ibn Hanbal, *al-Musnad*, V, 417, 418.

love, refined manners and kindness. Even after she died, when a sacrifice was made he always sent some of the meat to her relatives [2]. He had blessed memories of her.

The first twenty four years of the Prophet's life in marriage, the duration of which corresponds to his youth and period of highest energy, were spent only with Khadijah, may Allah be pleased with her. Most of his later wives were older than he and were widowed. The only virgin and young woman among these later wives was Aishah, may Allah be pleased with her. Aishah grasped the religious issues of women with intelligence and foresight. After the demise of the Prophet (peace be upon him), she continued to live for an extended period of time during which she enlightened both men and women with her broad knowledge. This body of knowledge later constituted one of the solid foundations of Islamic thought. The following account bears witness to how this goal was achieved: Abu Musa al-Ashari, one of the leading companions of the Prophet Muhammad (peace be upon him) said: "We, as the companions of the Prophet, asked Aishah whenever we faced a question about any hadith and we always found satisfactory knowledge in her answers."[3] Another reason behind this marriage was to confirm the intimacy between the Prophet (peace be upon him) and Abu Bakr (may Allah be pleased with him), who was "the second of the two" [4] in the cave of Thawr, as reported in the Qur'an.

✽

---

(2) Muslim, *Fadâil al-Sahâbah* 75; Ibn Hibbân, *al-Sahîh*, XV, 467.
(3) Tirmidhî, *Manâqıb* 62.
(4) See Holy Qur'an, Tawba, 9/ 40.

Prophet Muhammad, was elevated to the level of prophethood at the age of forty after leading a pure life during his youth and a sublime family life. Six months prior to the age of forty, Almighty Allah opened the cave of Hira to him, near Mecca, as a divine school.

In this spiritual classroom, where his sacred education continued in secrecy, he was given lessons about what is transient and eternal. Eventually, at the age of forty, he was endowed with the power to guide people and with the certificate of prophethood as the order came: *"Read: In the name of thy Lord Who created!"* (Qur'an, Alaq, 96/1-2).

The first six months after this blessing, perceived from the angle our minds may comprehend, were noteworthy for their "trustworthy dreams." In truth, Hira resembled the adventure of a seed beneath the soil, a place of spiritual formation which will remain veiled to humanity forever. Externally speaking, the factors that led Prophet Muhammad (peace be upon him) to the cave were his all-encompassing compassion and sorrow for the people of his time because of their misery and their heresy. In reality, this was the preparatory phase for the transfer of the Qur'an from the Divine presence to human understanding through the pure heart of Muhammad. It was the time for the development of his latent power to shoulder the heavy burden of revelation, which is impossible for ordinary people to carry. This is like the transformation of raw iron into steel by using its inner potential. It is impossible to imagine a mind that could come close to the essence of this secret or a discourse capable of penetrating it that would not shatter into pieces when touched by it.

Those who could not look at this world through the window of the heart constituted the miserable mob who gathered under the black flag of Abu Jahl and Abu Lahab, the two leading enemies of Islam in Mecca.

The life of the Prophet is full of divine manifestations of honor which had not been given to any previous prophets. Allah, the Most High, called only him as "my beloved" (*Habibi*). Likewise, he was the only one who was blessed with *Miraj* (i.e. ascension to the throne of Allah) [5].

His superiority became evident when he led all the previous prophets in prayer in Jerusalem before Miraj. The secret of *"len terani"* [6] in the life of Moses (peace be upon

---

(5) Bukhârî, *Salât* 1; Muslim, *Îmân* 259; Abû Dâwûd, *Sunnah* 23; Tirmidhî, *Tıb* 12; Ahmad ibn Hanbal, *al-Musnad*, III, 224.

(6) The secret of *"len terâni"* (You will never see me!): Moses (peace be upon him) was put through a stage of preparation with the purpose of preparing to talk to Allah. He was ordered to fast first for thirty days which was extended to forty by adding ten more days to the initial number. This period was a phase of preparation to talk to Allah by getting stripped of carnal desires. Moses (peace be upon him) talked to Allah not through material means such as tongue and language but through the eternal divine attribute of *Kalam*, speech. No one heard or felt this dialogue, not even the angel Gabriel or the seventy witnesses who came with Moses (peace be upon him). Yet, Moses (peace be upon him) fainted because of this divine manifestation. He lost his senses as to whether he was in this world or in the Hereafter and felt out of space and time. Drowned in love and ecstasy, a strong passion was aroused in him to see the Ultimate Truth, *al-Haqq*. In response, the divine answer came: "len terâni" (you will never see me!). As Moses (peace be upon him) insisted unknowingly, Allah said to him to look at the mountain. He let him know that if the mountain could endure the Divine manifestation, he could also endure it. Narrative has it that a small Divine light from behind endless veils leaked onto the mountain. The

him) showed itself as *"qaba qawsayni aw adna"* [7] in his life. In his religion, Islam, salat (prayer) which is the point of union with Allah, was offered to his Ummah as a blessing.

❀

After thirteen years of struggle guiding people, he was led to another cave. It was the Thawr cave on the Hijrah path. This cave was not for education but for drowning in the secrets of Allah and for perfecting the heart. The stay in this cave lasted for three days and nights. This time he was not alone. His companion was Abu Bakr, who is the highest, and spiritually the richest after the Prophet. Abu Bakr had the honor of being with the Prophet in the cave. He thus became the "second of the two." Prophet Muhammad, said to his noble friend:

"Have no fear, for Allah is with us" (Qur'an, Tawba, 9/40). In this way, he taught him how to be with Allah (mai'yyah). This was the first lesson in secret dhikr and in the satisfaction of the hearts by opening them to Allah.

In other words, the Thawr cave served as the first place

---

mountain shattered into pieces. Moses (peace be upon him) fainted from this frightening event. When he woke up, he praised Allah and repented for trying to cross his limits.

(7) *"Qaba qawsayni aw adna"* [Then he approached and came closer, and was at a distance of but two bow-lengths or (even) closer. Najm 8-9]: The Prophet (peace be upon him) was taken behind the Sidra al-Muntaha. Even Gabriel is not allowed to approach this close to Allah. The verse describes this distance as "two bow-lengths or (even) closer." A private and sacred union between the Prophet and Allah took place at this distance, which is impossible for the human mind to comprehend. This serves as a comparison between Moses and Muhammad (peace be upon them) presented to our humble and powerless minds.

in the primary education of the heart, which carries a servant to Allah in the boundless sky of secrets, and was also the first station on this sacred journey. At this time Prophet Muhammad (peace be upon him) began to disclose to Abu Bakr for the first time the secrets in his heart, which is a spring of light. The first link in the Golden Chain, which will last for eternity, was thus formed. Faith takes its power from love. The fundamental motive behind all sublime journeys is love for him. The only path to gain the blessing of Allah is through following his example. This is because the law of love commands to love not only the beloved but also what the beloved loves. It is not possible to comprehend such a divine love through our weak and inadequate understanding.

We believe that the following story will have an impact on every heart, depending on its horizons and capabilities. Abu Bakr Siddiq (the faithful), for his entire life, found a new and different joy and pleasure from all his conversations and friendship with the Prophet (peace be upon him). Familiar with the most intimate secrets of prophethood, and blessed with many manifestations, he used to long for the Prophet (peace be upon him) even while they were together.

When he heard Prophet Muhammad (peace be upon him) saying: "I have not benefited from the property of any one else more than I have benefited from the property of Abu Bakr," Abu Bakr (may Allah be pleased with him) responded in tears: "Aren't I and my property yours, O the Prophet!"[8]. He displayed that he had surrendered himself along with all

---

(8) Ibn Mâjah, *Fadâil Ashâb al-Nabî* 11; Ahmad ibn Hanbal, *al-Musnad*, II, 253; Ibn Hibbân, *al-Sahîh*, XV, 273; Ibn Abî 'Âsım, *al-Sunnah*, II, 577.

of his belongings to the Prophet (peace be upon him) and became "lost" (fani) in him. (This state is called "fana fi al-Rasul" [being lost in the Prophet] in tasawwuf). He spent all his wealth in the Prophet's path. For instance, once Prophet Muhammad (peace be upon him) said:

– Help the soldiers!

Abu Bakr brought all his wealth. When Prophet Muhammad (peace be upon him) asked him:

– What did you leave for your family and children?

He responded with great ecstasy of faith:

– Allah and His Prophet…! [9]

Muawiyah ibn Abi Sufyan said about him:

"The world did not want Abu Bakr; nor did he want the world…" [10]

It should be noted that Prophet Muhammad (peace be upon him) cared about Abu Bakr's family and did not want them to live in misery. Abu Bakr's (may Allah be pleased with him) donation of all his wealth constituted an exceptional circumstance among the companions. This may be due to the fact that Abu Bakr and his family had enduring patience and a strong reliance on Allah.

Allah was the helper, supporter, shelter and host of these two travelers. The unfaithful did not see anything but the web of a spider when they came to the entrance of the cave

---

(9) Tirmidhî, *Manâqıb* 16; Abû Dâwûd, *Zakât* 40; Dârimî, *Zakât* 26; al-Hâkim, *al-Mustadrak*, I, 574; al-Bayhaqî, *al-Sunan*, IV, 180; al-Bazzâr, *al-Musnad*, I, 263, 394.

(10) Ahmad ibn Hanbal, *Kitâb al-Zuhd*, p. 18.

where they were hiding themselves on Mount Thawr. After the Prophet and Abu Bakr entered the cave, a spider wove a web at the entrance of the cave which misled the unfaithful to think that there was no one inside the cave. As the poet Arif Nihat Asyali put it:

The spider's web was not in the air,
Neither was it in the water nor was it on the ground;
It was before the eyes
Of those who were blind to the truth. [11]

The two valuable travelers, under divine protection, reached Quba near Medina. As the honorable travelers who passionately had long been expected finally arrived, an atmosphere of joy and happiness prevailed over the entire city.

The fiery chanting of "Tala'al-badru 'alayna" (the full moon rose upon us) from the hills echoed in the sky and brought joy to the hearts. The date was the 12th of Rabi al-Awwal, and a new calendar was instituted for all posterity. All events from then on were going to be indexed to that day.

From that day forward, Medina became the center and the mirror for the development and for the spread of Islam. With the Hijrah, the dark face of disbelief (kufr) paled. The Prophet's Mosque in Medina and the Mosque of Quba acquired a sublime meaning and remained sacred places and souvenirs of this blessed Hijrah.

The Ansar (the Helpers) declared their wealth to the Muhajirun (the Immigrants): "This is my wealth; half of it is

---

(11) Asyalı, Arif Nihat, *Dualar ve Aminler*, (Istanbul, 1973), p.122

23

yours..." The groundwork of Islamic brotherhood, which is so hard for us to build through our limited forms of sacrifice and of giving, was thus established. With this, Medina attained its immortal place in Islamic history. It was in Medina that the Adhan, Ramadan, Eid, and Zakat became part of the Islamic life of the community and it was also in Medina that great historical battles took place. All these practices and events constituted ideal examples for the future of the entire Ummah.

The battle of Badr ended with the resistance and triumph of true faith over disbelief (kufr). Religious solidarity replaced traditional tribal solidarity. For instance, Abu Bakr (may Allah be pleased with him) encountered in battle his disbeliever son. Abu Ubayda ibn Jarrah (may Allah be pleased with him) similarly encountered his disbeliever father. Finally, Hamzah (may Allah be pleased with him) came face to face in battle with his disbeliever brother. They met each other with swords in their hands to fight. Such a fight over faith between people bound by blood ties was unimaginable before Islam; their battles being mostly fought over tribal disputes. Also the Highest Truth (Haqq Taala) sent an army of angels. These angels who joined in the flow of the sublime feelings gained more honor compared to other angels. After this great event, Allah the Highest revealed the following verse to protect the believers from self reliance and arrogance: *"It is not ye who slew them; it was Allah: When thou threwest (a handful) of dust), it was not thy act, but Allah's: In order that He might confer on the Believers a gracious benefit from Himself: for Allah is He who heareth and knoweth (all things)"* (Qur'an, Anfal, 8/17).

The battle of Uhud, which came after the battle of Badr, witnessed how the blood of Hamzah was shed. Including Hamzah, the number of martyrs reached to seventy. Ten martyrs at a time were brought for funeral prayers (salat al-janazah). Each time nine were buried, but Hamzah was the tenth individual and he was retained and included in all funeral services. Thus prayers were made repeatedly for Hamzah, who in his final state epitomized martyrdom. Let us not forget the Prophet loved his uncle with such depth that Hamzah was referred to by him as a part of his heart.

The battle of Uhud, which followed the battle of Badr was filled with frightening and sorrowful scenes such as those just cited. Through these tests the maturity of the community was evolving in terms of the believers' service to Allah and their submission to Him. The consequence of this growth produced the signature of that contentment with Allah's chosen destiny that is a mark of faith at its highest point.

In addition, an event that shook the heavens and the earth occurred when two rings from the shield of the Prophet pierced his cheek and broke one of his teeth. At that moment, all the companions were drowned in deep sorrow.

The Prophet (peace be upon him), wiped his blood with his hand from his face and did not let it fall on the ground, fearing that it may bring the wrath of Allah down on the earth. For the same reason, he was seeking refuge in Allah by praying thus:

"– O Allah! My community is ignorant about you. They

know not. Please give them guidance!" [12]

The hadith informs:

"The wrath of Allah increased against those who made the face of the Prophet bleed" [13]

Thus, Uhud housed such striking scenes.

The companions (Ashab) unconditionally followed the Prophet. They said to him:

"– O the Messenger of Allah! We believe in you. We have accepted with utmost sincerity the Qur'an which you brought to us from Allah. And we have made a covenant with you that we will obey you and follow you. Act the way you like, give us orders! We are always with you! By Allah who sent you to us, if you enter a sea we will also enter with you. None of us will refrain from doing so…" [14] They, when saying these words, were at the zenith of their joy of faith.

Yet, at Uhud, a moment of disobedience to an order of the Messenger of Allah and a slight inclination toward worldly gains altered the outcome of the war. The divine warning manifested itself and consequently the triumph was delayed.

On the other hand, Uhud is a mountain that had a distinguished place in the heart of the Messenger of Allah (peace be upon him). He continued all his life to visit Uhud

---

(12) Bukhârî, *Anbiyâ* 54; Muslim, *Jihâd* 104; Ibn Mâjah, *Fitan* 23; Ahmad ibn Hanbal, *al-Musnad*, I, 380.

(13) Ibn Ishâq, *Sîrah*, p. 311; Ahmad ibn Hanbal, *al-Musnad*, II, 317; Ibn Abî Shaybah, *al-Mosesnnaf*, VII, 373.

(14) Bukhârî, *Magâzî* 4; Muslim, *Jihâd* 83; Ahmad ibn Hanbal, *al-Musnad*, I, 389, 428, 457; Ibn Abî Shaybah, *al-Mosesnnaf*, VII, 66.

and the martyrs of Uhud. He used to repeatedly say: "We love Uhud and Uhud loves us!..." [15] These words have honored this place known for its martyrs' graves and for the special place it occupied in his heart as reflected in his practice of periodically visiting it. This site will always remain special.

❧

In the battle of Khandaq (trenches), the Prophet broke a huge rock which the companions were unable to crack. With the first hit, he said he saw the Palace of Caesar. With the second hit, he said he saw the Palace of Kisra, the Persian king. With the third hit, he said he saw the collapse of the palaces in San'ah, Yemen. Here, he was giving good tidings for the coming spread of Islam to these lands and thus he injected hope of prospective triumph into the hearts of the believers. He was giving good tidings that truth would prevail over falsehood and was drawing a map of the universe in which impossibilities would become possible one after another.

The battle of Khandaq contained abundant pain, fatigue, hunger, cold and darkness. The Messenger of Allah (peace be upon him) prayed:

"O my Lord! The real life is the life of the Hereafter. Please help the Helpers (*Ansar*) and the Immigrants (Muhajirun)." [16]

He was explaining in these prayers that all pain and

---

(15) Bukhârî, *İ'tisâm* 16; Muslim *Fadâil* 10; Ibn Mâjah, *Manâsik* 104; Muwatta, *Madînah* 10; Ahmad ibn Hanbal, *al-Musnad*, III, 140.

(16) Bukhârî, *Jihâd* 34; Abû Dâwûd, *Salât* 12; Nasâî, *Masâjid* 12; Ahmad ibn Hanbal, *al-Musnad*, VI, 289.

fatigue of this world are insignificant compared to the infinity of the Hereafter, and was thus directing his companions to the Hereafter as a goal.

❧

As was foretold by the Prophet at the time of the Hudaybiya Act, Muslims triumphed in subsequent battles and the people of Mecca opened their arms to its real owners. It had been conquered spiritually by its lovers with forgiveness, peace, security and guidance. The longing for Mecca, which was full of pain, oppression and hardship came to an end. The many years of sorrow turned into joy. Next, as a thanksgiving to Allah, the greatest scene of forgiveness in history was demonstrated. Many previous murderers of Muslims and many previous criminals gained the honor of Islam.

Eventually, the last verse was revealed in the Farewell Pilgrimage (Hajjat'ul-Wada'). It was made known that the religion was perfected. This, at the same time, was an implicit notice that the Prophet Muhammad (peace be upon him), who was sent as a mercy to the universe, had completed his task and the time was approaching for him to return to his Lord. As evidence of having taught the religion, he asked his companions to witness three times:

"O my companions! Did I convey the religion to you? Did I convey the religion to you? Did I convey the religion to you?"

As he received positive answers three times, he raised his hands, opened towards the heavens and asked Allah to witness. He said:

"Be the Witness, O Allah! Be the Witness, O Allah! Be the Witness, O Allah!" [17]

On this occasion, the sacred trust which was invested in the Prophet by Allah during the previous twenty three years in Mecca and Medina was transferred to the responsibility of the Ummah until the Day of Judgement.

Since the Prophet (peace be upon him) conquered his homeland and birth place, some of the Helpers (Ansar) began to voice their concern:

"Allah the Most High opened Mecca to his Prophet. From now on, he will stay in Mecca and will not return to Medina."

Although this was an intimate conversation among themselves, the Messenger of Allah later told them about their concern. They became embarrassed and confessed their conversation. Rasulullah (peace be upon him) said to the Ansar:

"I seek refuge in Allah from doing that! My life and death will be with you..." [18]

He displayed an example of unparalleled loyalty and returned to Medina.

❊

---

(17) Bukhârî, *Fitan* 8; Muslim, *Îmân* 378; Abû Dâwûd, *Manâsik* 56; Nasâî, *İhdâs* 4; Ibn Mâjah, *Fitan* 2; Dârimî, *Manâsik* 34; Ahmad ibn Hanbal, *al-Musnad*, I, 447.

(18) Muslim, *Jihâd* 86; Ahmad ibn Hanbal, *al-Musnad*, II, 538; Ibn Hibbân, *al-Sahîh*, XI, 75; Nasâî, *al-Sunan al-Kubrâ*, VI, 382; al-Bayhaqî, *al-Sunan al-Kubrâ*, IX, 117.

Adam (peace be upon him) to whom angels were ordered to prostrate;

Elijah (peace be upon him) who beheld the secrets of the heavens;

Noah (peace be upon him) who cleansed the earth with the flood;

Hud (peace be upon him) who turned the lands of disbelief upside down with storms;

Salih (peace be upon him) who shook the foundations of the houses of disobedience and rebellion;

Abraham (peace be upon him) who turned the fire of Nimrod into a rose garden by his submission and reliance on Allah;

Ishmael (peace be upon him) who is the symbol of sincerity, loyalty, reliance and submission to Allah and whose stories will be remembered by believers during the Pilgrimage until the Day of Judgement;

Isaac, (peace be upon him) from whose progeny came the prophets of Israel;

Lot (peace be upon him), the sad prophet of the people of Sodom and Gomorra, who took their place in the garbage yard of history as they were erased from the face of the earth because of their excessive immorality and rebellion;

Zulkarnayn (peace be upon him) who carried the torch of Tawhid (faith in the unity of God) from the east to the west;

Jacob (peace be upon him) who was a statue of patience, love and longing;

Joseph (peace be upon him) whose beauty made the beauty of the moon fade and who became the sultan of Egypt after he went through a period of slavery, loneliness in prison, living as a stranger, trial, pain, hardship, and struggle against passions;

Shuayb (peace be upon him) who is called the orator of the prophets and who filled hearts with ecstasy by virtue of his sermons;

Khidir (peace be upon him) who taught the divine secrets to Moses;

Moses (peace be upon him) who destroyed the hegemony of the Pharaoh and who opened a path in the Red Sea with his rod;

Aaron (peace be upon him) who helped his brother Moses (peace be upon him) at all times and in all places;

David (peace be upon him) who with his prayers (dhikr), put the mountains, stones and wild animals in ecstasy;

Suleiman (peace be upon him) whose heart refused to assign value to his glorious kingdom.

Uzayr (peace be upon him) who became the example of resurrection on the Day of Judgment as he was resurrected after being dead for a hundred years;

Ayyub (peace be upon him) who became the grindstone of patience;

Yunus (peace be upon him) who overcame darkness by going deeper in dhikr, supplication and penitence while in a state of great ecstasy;

31

Ilyas (peace be upon him) who attained the divine blessing when he was greeted by Allah: *"Peace and salutation to such as Ilyas"* (Qur'an, Saffat, 37/130).

Elijah (peace be upon him) who was elevated over the worlds;

The pure hearted prophet Zulkifl (peace be upon him) who was showered by divine blessing;

Lukman (peace be upon him) the leader of doctors of internal and external health, who became a legendary figure with his insightful advice;

The oppressed prophet Zakariyya (peace be upon him) who maintained his submission to and reliance on Allah even when his body was divided into two pieces without screaming "aah!"!

John (peace be upon him) who, like his father, faced death as a martyr;

The heavenly exalted Jesus (peace be upon him) whose distinct qualities included purity of soul, healing the ill, giving life to the dead by seeking the help of Allah through sincere supplication;

In total, approximately one hundred and twenty thousand prophets along with the flow of divine manifestations and occurrences in their lives descended on the spiritual soil of humanity like the clouds of April after they reach the level of saturation. Those prophets who had been the blessed sparks of divine guidance, and who through their examples and messages had functioned as a chain of prophecy, served as good tidings of spring foretelling the emergence of Muhammad Mustafa (peace be upon him) who was to be sent as a mercy to the worlds...

❀

Our sources tell us that the lucky woman Suwayba was one of the milk mothers of the Messenger of Allah. She was the slave girl of Abu Lahab.

The lady Suwayba was also the first to give good tidings of the birth of his nephew to Abu Lahab. As a consequence of this good news arriving through her, he set her free out of his tribal spirit and happiness. This event took place on a Monday. The happiness of Abu Lahab for the birth of Muhammad (peace be upon him), even though it was mixed in a mundane way with feelings of tribal solidarity, will cause the punishment of this disbeliever in the Hellfire to decrease on Mondays.

After his death some saw Abu Lahab in a dream and asked him about his life in the Hereafter:

– "Abu Lahab! How are you?"

– "I am being punished in the Hellfire! Yet my punishment lessens on Monday nights. I suck between my fingers on that night. Water comes and I feel cold by drinking it. This is because on that day I set Suwayba free as she ran to me and gave me the good tidings about the birth of the Messenger of Allah. In return, Allah rewarded me by decreasing my punishment on Monday nights."

Ibn al-Jazari said:

"A disbeliever like Abu Lahab benefited from his display of happiness on the occasion of the birth of the Prophet even though it was mixed with tribal feelings. Comparatively, imagine the kind of divine gifts and blessings a true believer acquires if he, out of respect for that night, opens his heart to the Eternal Pride of the World and his table to guests..." The appropriate way of celebrating the birth of the Prophet is to organize, during the month in which the Prophet was born, recurrent conferences to rekindle the light of the heart. The purpose of these acts is to benefit from the spirituality of this blessed month while giving feasts for the Ummah; to make content the sad hearts of the poor, the stranger, the orphan and the helpless by helping in various ways and by giving them charity; and to organize recitations of Qur'an in public. [19]

❀

This orphan was unlettered because he had never taken lessons, yet he came as the savior of all humanity, the interpreter of the unseen world and the teacher of the school of Truth.

Moses (peace be upon him) brought rules and regulations. David was distinguished by chanting supplications and invocations. The sublime Jesus was sent to teach humanity, the most beautiful manners, and asceticism from the material world. The Prophet of Islam, Muhammad, (peace be upon him), nevertheless, brought all these: he instituted rules and taught how to purify the soul and to worship Allah with a clean heart. He instructed humanity in the best morality and represented it in his life. He identified

---

(19) Joseph ibn Ismâîl al-Nabhânî, *al-Anwâr al-Muhammadiyyah min al-mawâhib al-ladunniyah*, p. 28-29 (Some part of this riwayah was narrated by al-San'ânî, *al-Mosesnnaf*, VII, 478; al-Bayhaqî, *Shu'ab al-Îmân*, I, 261; al-Marwazî, *al-Sunnah*, I, 82; İbn Hagar al-'Asqalânî, *Fath al-Bârî*, IX, 145).

how not to be cheated by the false attractions of this world. In brief, he gathered in his personality and work the capacity and obligations of all the Prophets. Dignity out of both family genealogy and high morality, blissfulness out of both perfect character and physical beauty were all gathered in him.

When he reached the age of forty, this was undoubtedly a turning point for humanity.

He lived for forty years among people. Most of the splendid things he was to bring were yet unknown to them. He was not known as statesman, nor preacher nor public speaker. Apart from being reputed as a triumphant commander, he was not known even as a regular soldier.

He had never given a speech about the history of past nations, the prophets, the Day of Judgement, nor Paradise nor the Hellfire. He was alone in an exclusively sublime life and moral state. Yet, he changed completely after he came down from the cave in the Mountain of Hira with a divine commandment.

All of Arabia was shocked and frightened as he began his mission. His extraordinary speech and discourse enchanted all of them. Public competitions of poetry, literature, rhetoric and discourse suddenly came to an end. Poets no longer dared to post their poems on the wall of the Holy Ka'bah. This tradition, centuries long, thus ended, to the extent that even the daughter of the most famous Arab poet, Imru'ul-Qays, was so thrilled after listening to a passage from the Qur'an, that she said in great surprise:

– "This cannot be the word of a human! If there is such a

word in the world, my father's poems must be taken off from the walls of the Ka'bah. Go and pull them down; and in their place post these verses...!"

❀

He challenged the entire world to produce chapters similar to the chapters of the Qur'an. Yet, the challenge of the Qur'an, at that time, to produce an equivalent to one of its chapters found no response even until today.

Allah says:

"And if you are in doubt as to what We have revealed from time to time to our servant, then produce a chapter like thereunto; And call your witnesses or helpers (if there is any) besides Allah, if you are truthful" (Qur'an, Baqara, 2/23).

❀

This unlettered man, who came out of an uncivilized society, made the people of his time powerless as a result of the mass of knowledge and wisdom revealed through him within a sea of miracles that will not be surpassed until the last day. This fact is proven in different ways. Although the Holy Qur'an touches upon many academic and scientific issues, as well as predictions about future events, none of what was revealed has been contradicted by new scientific discoveries. In contrast, respected encyclopedias feel obliged to publish every year a new volume to rectify their mistakes by updating the information in their previous edition.

Prophet Muhammad (peace be upon him) personally taught all of humanity that he was the vicegerent of the Truth (al-Haqq) on the earth.

He laid down the basic principles of social, cultural, and economic organization, the basic principles of government and international relations and did this in ways which may only be understood through life long research on the material and immaterial worlds by the most distinguished scholars of our time. Indeed, humanity will better comprehend the reality of Muhammad (peace be upon him) as it develops in the areas of theoretical knowledge and practical experience.

Prophet Muhammad (peace be upon him) –even though he had never carried a sword, had never gone through military training, and had never participated in a campaign except once as a witness– proved to be a great soldier who never gave up even in the most challenging battles engaged in during the struggle to spread faith in the oneness of God. He had to do this for peace in his society despite an endless mercy that encompassed the whole of humanity. In nine years, he conquered all of Arabia with his comparatively weak military. He achieved miraculous success in providing spiritual power and military training to the undisciplined and unorganized people of his time. His achievements reached to the extent that his followers militarily defeated the two most powerful of the empires of that time, namely the Byzantine and the Persian Empires. Thus was realized the good tidings which he had given years ago in Mecca:

The Prophet (peace be upon him) said to the people of Mecca;

– "Accept the religion and follow me!"

Abu Jahl objected:

– "Even if we follow you, the tribes of Mudar and Rabi'a will not obey you anyway!"

The Prophet responded to him:

– " Willingly or unwillingly, not only they, but also the Persians and the Byzantine people will follow me!" [20]

This promise was soon realized.

Despite all the negative conditions, the Messenger of Allah brought about the greatest world revolution in human history, silenced the oppressors, and put an end to the tears of the oppressed. His fingers used to serve as a comb for the hair of the orphans. With his comforting, hearts were relieved of their anxieties.

Mehmed Akif, the famous Turkish poet, illustrated this scene in an excellent way:

Suddenly the orphan grew up and reached forty,
The bloody feet stepping on the heads reached the water!
With a sole breath, this innocent saved humanity,
With one movement, he defeated the Caesars and Kisras,
The weak, who used to deserve only oppression, stood up,
The oppressors, who never expected demise, vanished,
.. mercy to the worlds was indeed his enlightening religion,
With his wings, he covered the country of those who asked for justice,

---

(20) Ibn Ishâq, *Sirah*, p.190 (Similar narratives are found in, Ahmad b. Hanbal, *al-Musnad*, IV, 128; al-Hâkim, *al-Mustadrak*, III, 728; al-Bayhaqî, *al-Sunan al-Kubrâ*, IX, 31; Ibn Abî Shaybah, *al-Mosesnnaf*, VI, 311; Ma'mar ibn Râshid, *al-Jâmi'*, XI, 48).

What the world owns is only gifts from him,
Society is indebted to him, individuals are indebted to him,
Indebted to this innocent one is the whole humanity,
O Lord! With this confession, resurrect us on the Last Day,

If Prophet Muhammad, who gathered in his personality all virtues, had not come to the world, humanity would have remained in oppression and wildness, and the weak would have been enslaved by the powerful until the end of time. The balance of the world would have changed in favor of evil. In such a circumstance, the world would be dominated by oppressors and it would belong only to the powerful few. How nicely, the poet describes this situation:

O the Messenger of Allah! If you had not come to the world,
Roses would not have bloomed, the nightingale would not have chanted,
The names of God would have remained unknown to humanity,
Existence would lose its meaning and be drawn into grief!..

❀

He conducted twenty seven battles and approximately fifty raids called "sariyya". Islam was firmly established with the conquering of Mecca. Allah declared in the following verse of the Qur'an that Islam is the highest level of human perfection:

"This day, have I perfected your religion for you, completed my favor upon you, and have chosen for you Islam as your religion" (Qur'an, Maida, 5/3).

It was time for the greatest separation and union.

A day before his illness, he went to the graveyard of Medina, which is called Jannat'ul-Baqi', where he prayed for the diseased as follows:

– "O Allah, the Greatest! Please do not refrain from pardoning the people who lie here." [21]

With this act, he looked as if he was bidding farewell to them.

After returning from the graveyard, it was time to bid farewell to his companions. He gave them the following advice:

– "Allah, the Most High, gave a choice to one of his servants between this world and its attractions and the blessings in Paradise. The servant chose what is in Paradise..."

Hearing these words, Abu Bakr (may Allah be pleased with him) who had a sensitive heart felt that the Prophet (peace be upon him) was saying good-bye to them. A great grief covered him, his heart saddened, and tears gushed from his heart and eyes. He wept sobbingly:

– May my father and mother be sacrificed for your sake, O Messenger of Allah! Let us sacrifice for you our souls, the soul of our fathers, mothers and children, and our property..."

No one else in the congregation understood the deeply hidden message of the Prophet and sensed the feelings of Prophet Muhammad, peace and greetings be upon him. This was because Abu Bakr was "the second of the two" in the cave of Thawr. [22]

---

(21) Muslim, *Janâiz* 102; Nasâî, *Janâiz* 103; Ibn Hibbân, *al-Sahîh,* VII, 444.

(22) Bukhârî, *Salât* 80; Muslim, *Fadâil al-Sahâbah* 2; Tirmidhî, *Manâqıb* 15; Dârimî, *Muqaddimah* 14; Nasâî, *Janâiz* 69; Ahmad ibn Hanbal, *al-Musnad,* III, 18.

The sensitive and refined heart of Abu Bakr, however, intuitively understood the holy and great farewell and commenced to scream like a reed flute who cries out of separation.

The daughter of the Prophet, our blessed Mother Fatimah, the leader of the women in Paradise, became so sad from the temporary separation from her father, the Prophet of Mercy to the worlds (peace be upon him), that she said:

– "As Prophet Muhammad (peace be upon him) went to the Hereafter, a great grief fell upon me. It was so great that if it had fallen on daylight it would have turned to night." [23]

He left two great guides to us, the Holy Qur'an and the Sunnah.

The Holy Qur'an and the Sunnah are two eternal souvenirs of Prophet Muhammad and the prescriptions for the happiness in this world and the Hereafter.

After his return to Medina, following a bitter illness that lasted for thirteen days, the horizons of beauty were opened to his soul. The date was the 8th of June, 632 or the 12th of Rabi'ul-awwal in the 11th year of the Hijra calendar.

Between the two shoulder blades of the Prophet, there was a divine sign indicating that he was the last Prophet. Most of the companions desired to kiss it. Imam Bayhaqi stated that:

"The Blessed companions doubted whether the Prophet (peace be upon him) really traveled to the Hereafter as they saw no changes in his face after he immigrated to the eternal world.

---

(23) al-Nabhânî, *al-Anwâr al-Muhammadiyyah min al-mawâhib al-ladunniyah*, p. 593.

Asma (may Allah be pleased with her) searched for the sign of prophethood in his body. As they saw that it disappeared, it was determined, for certain, that he passed to the next world" [24]

The religion was perfected; the approval of the companions of the transfer of the divine message to humanity was demonstrated and was presented as witness to the Most High Truth (al-Haqq). Following this, Prophet Muhammad was invited to the world of eternity.

Presently, he is waiting for his Ummah by the Mahshar, that is the square of resurrection, on the Sirat and the river of Kawthar.

Grant us your intercession, O Rasulullah!

Help us, O Rasulullah!

Welcome us, O Rasulullah!

❊

The world was blessed by his birth on Monday the 12th of Rabi al-awwal.

Allah gave him the task of serving as a Prophet on Monday the 12th of Rabi al-awwal. Abu Qatada narrated as follows:

"Prophet Muhammad was asked about fasting on Mondays. In response he said:

– This is the day on which I was born and was sent as a Prophet". [25]

---

(24) Ibn Sa'd, *al-Tabakât*, II, 271; al-Bayhaqî, *Dalâil al-nubuwwah*, VII, 219.

(25) Muslim, *Sıyâm* 196; Ahmad ibn Hanbal, *al-Musnad*, V, 299; Ibn Hibbân, *al-Sahîh*, VIII, 403; al-Bayhaqî, *al-Sunan al-Kubrâ*, IV, 286.

Likewise, on Monday the 12th of Rabi al-awwal, he entered Medina and laid the ground stone for the new Islamic State which will last forever.

And finally, again on Monday the 12th of Rabi al-awwal, he immigrated to the Hereafter.

As an exemplification of a divine manifestation, his birth, his Hijra from Mecca to Medina and his transit from this world to the Next World, through the majesty of Allah all took place on Monday the 12th of Rabi al-Awwal. This is a confirmation of the holiness of this month. The manifestations of Divine Beauty (Jamal) and Divine Glory (Jalal) are richly experienced at this time. In the inner worlds, the joys of a festival along with the pains of a separation are intertwined in the union of these two opposites. He is, yet again with mercy and compassion, waiting for his Ummah in the Hereafter.

With the travel of the Prophet of Allah to the World of Happiness, this world became deprived of his physical presence. Indeed, it is a disloyal world as expressed in the poetry of the Ottoman Sufi Poet, Aziz Mahmud Hudayi:

Who expects loyalty from you?
Are not you the fake world?
Are not you the same earth,
That took away Muhammad Mustafa? [26]

---

(26) Hudâî, Mahmud, *Kulliyyât-ı Hudâî*, (Istanbul, 1338), p. 109.

HIS EXEMPLARY LIFE
AND PLACE
AMONG THE PROPHETS

"Light upon Light." **(Qur'an, al-Nur, 24/35)**

The lifestyle of the Prophet is the best example for each and every human being. He is the best example of a religious leader. He is the finest example of a state leader. He is the example to follow for those who enter the garden of divine love. He is the highest example of gratitude and humbleness for those who are showered with the gifts of God. He is the greatest example of patience and submission, in the most challenging times and places. He is the best example of generosity and heedlessness towards collecting bounty. He is the finest example of compassion towards the family. His is the greatest example of mercy towards the weak, the lonely and the slaves and he is exemplary in pardoning the guilty.

If you are wealthy, contemplate the humbleness and generosity of Prophet Muhammad, who gained the hearts of the leaders who controlled all of Arabia!...

If you are weak, adopt the example of the Prophet during the period he spent in Mecca under the rule of the oppressive and usurping polytheists.

47

If you are a triumphant conqueror, take your example from the life of the courageous Prophet who defeated his enemies in Badr and Hunayn.

If you lose a battle, may Allah protect you, and in that case, remember the example of the Prophet who walked with dignity, courage and reliance on Allah, among his martyred and wounded companions after the battle of Uhud.

If you are a teacher, contemplate the example of the Prophet who taught God's orders by conveying his soft and sensitive enlightenment to the people of Suffa (Ashab al-Suffa) in the school at his Mosque.

If you are a student, bring to mind the example of the Prophet who sat on his knees before the Archangel, the Trustworthy Gabriel (Jibril al-Amin).

If you are a preacher or a sincere spiritual guide (murshid) for people, listen to the voice of the Prophet, who spread wisdom to his companions.

If you aim to defend the truth, convey it to others and lift it up, yet you do not even have a helper in this matter, then look at the life of the Prophet who proclaimed the truth in Mecca against the oppressors while inviting them to it.

If you defeated your enemies, broke their resistance and triumphed over them, destroyed the superstitions and declared the truth, then imagine the example of the Prophet on the day he conquered Mecca. He entered this holy city as a triumphant commander, yet with great humbleness, sitting on his camel as if he were in the state of sajdah; that is prostration to God, as an expression of gratitude to Allah.

If you are a farmer, take your example from the Prophet

whom, after conquering the lands of Bani Nadr, Khyabar and Fadak, choose excellent people to develop and manage these lands in the most productive way.

If you are lonely, with no relatives, bring to mind the example of the orphan of Abdullah and Aminah, their most beloved and only innocent son.

If you are an adolescent, pay attention to the life of the Prophet who, as a young man and candidate for prophethood, served in Mecca as a shepherd for the sheep of his uncle Abu Talib.

If you are a business man and travelling for trade, think about the experiences of the Most Honored Person, Muhammad (peace be upon him) while leading the caravan going from Mecca to Syria and Busra.

If you are a judge or a referee, bring to mind his justice and foresight when he solved the conflict among the tribes of Mecca over the prestige of putting back the Black Stone (Hagar al-Aswad) as they were on the verge of killing each other.

Again, turn your eyes to history and consider the example of the Prophet as he, in his Masjid in Medina, treated equally the poor in distress and the wealthy, as he judged between them with utmost balance.

If you are a husband, look carefully at the pure life style, the compassion and the deep feelings of the Prophet as an examplary husband.

If you are a parent, learn about the example of the father of Fatimah al-Zahra, and the grandfather of Hasan and Husayn in his manners towards them.

Regardless of your qualities and the state you are in, day or night, you will find him as the most perfect role model, teacher and guide for yourself.

He is so perfect a teacher that through following his example you can correct all your mistakes, eliminate chaos from your life and bring order to your life. Through his light and guidance, you can overcome the difficulties of life and attain real happiness.

As a matter of fact, his life is a bouquet composed of the rarest and the most elegant flowers and roses with the finest of fragrances.

❀

If you observe justice prevailing over the world, if there is affection binding together the rich and the poor, if the wealthy in a society treat the poor compassionately by offering them timely help, if the strongest protect the oppressed, if the healthy aid the ill, if the owners of wealth take good care of the orphans and feed the widows, then, be sure that all these virtuous acts have been inherited from Prophets and their followers.

This fact is more observable in the life of Prophet Muhammad, peace and greetings be upon him. This is because he is the zenith of prophethood. Even impartial, non-Muslims feel obliged to accept and appreciate his perfection. The English historian, Thomas Carlyle expressed his views about the Prophet in his book, *On Heroes, Hero-Worship and the Heroic in History,* [1] where he chose the best

---

(1) Carlyle, Thomas; *On Heroes, Hero-Worship and the Heroic in History;* University of Nebraska Press, 1966.

people in various professions and analyzed their lives and work. For instance, Carlyle identifies who deserves to be called the best poet, who deserves to be called the best commander, etc. Carlyle, a Christian who confesses his faith in his book, determined, described and analyzed Prophet Muhammad (peace be upon him) as the best among the prophets.

In the middle of this century in Lahey, Holland, a group of prominent scholars and thinkers determined who were the hundred greatest people in world history, and they felt obliged to choose Prophet Muhammad (peace be upon him) as the number one person on the list.

The real virtue is the one which is accepted and appreciated even by the opponents... The virtue and wisdom of Prophet Muhammad (peace be upon him) is accepted even by those who do not believe in him. This is because the exceptional personality of Prophet Muhammad (peace be upon him) gathered in itself the moral perfection that can respond to various situations separately. Only his life-example (sirah) can serve as a model to be followed by people from different stages and states of life. He constitutes the starting point for the education of humanity all over the world. He sprinkles light on the path of those who search for light. His guidance is an enlightening and never misguiding light for all who look for the right path. He is the sole guide of all of humanity.

The people who sat in his circle for guidance constituted a universe in which all kinds of people gathered. All nations, in spite of the differences in their languages, colors and types as well as the diversity of their social and cultural levels, united in that circle. There was no restriction, no exclusion of any one from the circle. It was like a feast of wisdom and knowledge that is not exclusive to a race but approaches humans only from the angle of humanness. Thus there was no difference between the weak and the strong.

Consider the followers of our master, Prophet Muhammad; you will see the following distinguished figures: Najashi, the king of Abyssinia of that time, Farwa, the leader of Ma'an, Zulkilah, the leader of Himyar, Daylami of Firuz, Marakabud who was from the leaders of Yemen, Ubayd and Jafar from the governors of Umman.

With another look, you will notice, besides kings and notable leaders, the slaves and the poor people who had no one, such as Bilal, Yasir, Habbab, Ammar and Abu Fukayha as well as the slave girls and women without supporters such as Sumayya, Lubayna, Zinnira, Nahdiyya and Umm Abis.

Among his honorable companions, there were people with superior minds, bright ideas and strong opinions along with people who were skilled in the most delicate works, who had a deep understanding of the secrets of the world and who had the ability to manage countries with wisdom and power.

Followers of the Prophet (peace be upon him) governed cities. They ruled provinces. People attained happiness through them. They experienced the taste of justice. People spread peace and tranquility among them. Human beings treated each other as brothers.

Lafayette who laid the intellectual foundations of the 1789 French Revolution, examined all existing legal systems before the proclamation of the Human Rights Declaration and realized the superiority of Islamic law which he distinctly expressed as follows:

"O Muhammad! No one else showed the level you reached in establishing justice!.."

❅

The character and the spiritual strength of the Prophet (peace be upon him) was so powerful that it elevated a previously semi-savage society who were unaware of human history to the stature of the companions, which is beyond the reach of others. He united them under one religion, flag, law, culture, civilization and government.

He turned uncultivated and lawless people into educated human beings, savages into civilized people, criminals and mean characters into God-conscious people; that is, extraordinary humans who lived in the awe and love of Allah.

A society which had not raised a notable figure for centuries produced many personalities ornamented with light and guidance. And they carried their enlightenment to the remote corners of the world; each as a torch of faith, knowledge and wisdom. The light that descended in the desert was distributed to the entirety of humanity. The purpose of the creation of the world was realized.

Although he conquered the hearts of people as the ideal teacher, a position he reached in a short while that the kings of this world cannot reach, he continued his previous humble life, ignoring the mundane bounties that became easily available to him. As before, he lived as one of the poor in his humble dwelling built with sun-dried bricks. He slept on a thin quilt stuffed with date leaves. He dressed modestly. He kept his standard of living below the standard of the poorest. At times, he could not find food and he had to tie a stone to his belly to suppress gnawing hunger, while, at the same time, showing gratefulness to Allah. He continued his supplication and worship although his past and future sins were all forgiven. He spent the night praying to such an extent that his feet became swollen. He immediately reached the poor with assistance when it was called for. He was a source of happiness for the miserable and the lonely. He personally spent time with the most helpless people despite his greatness. Furthermore, he protected them more than others with his endless compassion and tenderness.

On the day he conquered Mecca, where he was regarded by people as the most powerful man, one of his countryman approached him. He asked trembling:

– O Messenger of Allah! Teach me Islam!

He invited the man to relax by reminding him of the weakest point in his own life:

– Relax my brother! I am not a king, nor an emperor! I am the orphan of your old neighbor [meaning his mother] who used to eat sun-dried meat!.. [2]

With these words, he endowed to history the zenith of humility, the level of which has not been attained by others.

---

(2) Ibn Mâjah, *At'imah* 30; al-Hâkim, *al-Mustadrak*, II, 506; al-Tabarânî, *al-Mu'jam al-Awsat*, II, 64.

The same day, Abu Bakr, who was his friend in the cave during the Hijra, brought his father on his back because he was too old to walk. He wanted his father to be directly exposed to the message of the Prophet (peace be upon him). The Prophet (peace be upon him) said:

– O Abu Bakr! Why did you cause inconvenience to your old father? Could I not we go where he was? [3]

❀

Many countries entered willingly under his protection. His rule spread all over the Arabia. He could do everything he wished, yet he never compromised his humility. He said he did not have power over anything. He declared that everything is controlled by the power of Allah. Occasionally, he became wealthy. Caravans of camels flooded Medina with wealth. He distributed all that wealth to the poor and continued his humble life as before. He said:

"If I owned gold equal to the mountain of Uhud, I would not keep it more than three days except for my debts" [4].

Days used to pass without a fire burning in the house of the Prophet for cooking. Many times, he slept hungry.

One day, Umar came to the blessed house of the Prophet. He gazed at the room. It was almost empty. There was a mat woven from date leaves. The Prophet (peace be upon him) was sleeping on it. The dry leaves of the straw-mat left their prints on his blessed body. There was some barley flower in

---

(3) Ahmad ibn Hanbal, *al-Musnad*, VI, 349; Ibn Hibbân, *al-Sahîh*, XVI, 187; al-Hâkim, *al-Mustadrak*, III, 48.
(4) Bukhârî, *Tamannî* 2; Muslim, *Zakât* 31; Ibn Mâjah, *Zuhd* 8; Ahmad ibn Hanbal, *al-Musnad*, II, 256.

a corner. Next to it, there was a water container. Nothing else was in the room. His wealth consisted of these items at such a time when all Arabia bowed before his power. Umar sighed when he saw the situation. He could not keep himself from crying. As tears came from Umar's eyes, the Prophet asked:

– Why do you cry, O Umar?

Umar replied:

– Why should I not cry? O Messenger of Allah! The emperors of Rome and Iran are swimming in comfort! Yet, Rasulullah is sleeping on a simple mat filled with date leaves!

Prophet Muhammad (peace be upon him) comforted Umar and said to him:

– O Umar! Let the Ceasar and the emperor of Iran (Kisra) enjoy this world! The enjoyment of the Hereafter is enough for us!... [5].

In a similar incident, he said:

– What has this world to do with me? My relationship to this world is analogous to a traveler who travels on a summer day, sleeps under the shadow of a tree, then wakes up and goes his way [6]

His approach to life was a perfect one.

His life has been a perfect example for all his followers, be they rich or poor, strong or weak.

---

(5) Ahmad ibn Hanbal, *al-Musnad*, II, 298; al-Tabarânî, *al-Mu'jam al-Kabîr*, X, 162.

(6) Tirmidhî, *Zuhd* 44; Ibn Mâjah, *Zuhd* 3; Ahmad ibn Hanbal, *al-Musnad*, I, 301.

When he died, he did not own a single dirham or a dinar, nor a slave nor a sheep. What he left behind consisted of a white female mule, a sword and some land in Fadak which he had endowed as charity. That is to say, he did not leave property. Furthermore, since he was concerned that Muslims would give charity to those of his household, he prohibited them from accepting it.

These examples exhibit that this unlettered person who was born in an uncivilized world is the true leader of all times past, present and future, and his example is beyond imitation.

He did not give any value to wealth, luxury, kingdom, fame, comfort. While he was struggling to establish faith in the One God (tawhid), the wealth and glory of this world appeared to him as rubbish.

Aishah narrated that a woman from the Ansar visited her. When she saw that the bed of the Prophet (peace be upon him) was a simple mat, which was folded and put aside in the room, she ran to her home and came back with a nice bed which was stuffed with wool. Later, when the Prophet (peace be upon him) saw that his bed had been changed for a more comfortable one, he expressed his dislike and said to his wife, Aishah:

– O Aishah! Return this bed to its owner! By God, if I had wanted, God would have put under my control mountains of gold and silver able to walk with me in company [7].

This example alone is sufficient to demonstrate that the Prophet (peace be upon him) never attached any value to this world.

---

(7) Ahmad ibn Hanbal, *Kitâb al-Zuhd*, p. 53; al-Bayhaqî, *Shu'ab al-Îmân*, II, 173; Ibn Abî 'Âsım, *Kitâb al-Zuhd*, I, 14.

Besides these extraordinary attributes, one of his most distinguished qualities was his legendary love for his community (ummah), which is suitably illustrated by the following verse:

"Now hath come unto you, a messenger from amongst yourselves; it grieves him that you should suffer, ardently anxious is he over you; to the believers is the most kind and merciful" (Qur'an, Tawba, 9/128).

The blessed personality of the Prophet (peace be upon him), even in so far as the meager amount the human mind can grasp, which is not more than the tip of the iceberg, constitutes the zenith of the constellation of human behavior. This is because Allah the Most High created this blessed being as the *"uswa hasanah"*, the most perfect example for humanity to follow. Consequently, He elevated His Prophet (peace be upon him) by carrying him through stages, beginning with being an "orphan child" which is considered the lowest level of power in a society, and taking up him through all stages of life to the highest point of power and capacity, that is to prophethood and the leadership of the state. The purpose of this gradual elevation was to permit people of different levels of social stratification to take perfect examples of behavior from him and integrate them in accordance with their ability and power. Our people, who grasped this point very well, produced the grammatically belittled form (ism-i tasghir) of the name Muhammad and used it as a common name for everyone. This form of the name Muhammad in Turkish is Mehmetjik, which means little Muhammad. The noun Mehmetjik (the little Muhammad) brings to mind a small model of the Prophet (peace be upon him) in each human being, especially those who believe in the oneness of Allah and obey him. Or, with this attribution, it encourages every one to become like Muhammad (peace be upon him) within his or her own abilities.

❀

Even as a child or young man, no imperfection was observed in the personality of Prophet Muhammad (peace be upon him)–unlike other people who claimed to be the guides and leaders of humanity, primarily the philosophers. His personality did not develop through gradual perfection and improvement, which is the case with other leaders and guides. This was a result of divine destiny and support. He, even in childhood, displayed perfect manners which showed his merit for the responsibility he was to be charged with in the future.

The positive or negative views of philosophers, whose minds are not guided by divine revelation, about social peace and harmony, have remained for the most part on the pages of their books while the few that were translated into life were short-lived. Beyond this, philosophers failed to be concrete examples or models in their own lives or to provide examples in the lives of others of the principles they outlined about the perfection of human behavior.

The behavior of the Prophet (peace be upon him), however, functions as the practical criterion of morality and constitutes a perfect constellation of models. For instance, the philosopher Nietzsche expressed his view about super humans, but he could not explicate this concept of the extraordinary human with real actions taking place in every day life. Thus, it remained only in theory. In Islamic morality, however, the Prophet (peace be upon him) served and will continue to serve as the guide of humanity with all his actions as a human, which constitute the zenith of perfection.

Aristotle, on the other hand, outlined the principles and the laws of ethics. Yet, we cannot find anyone who attained happiness by faithfully applying Aristotle's philosophy. This is because the hearts of philosophers do not undergo a process of purification and cleansing as in the case of prophets, and their words and deeds are not perfected by the support of revelation. For this reason, their systems remain in conference rooms and on the pages of books, not in the daily lives of humans.

Our master, Prophet Muhammad (peace be upon him), however, before he took over the task of prophethood, gained the sympathy and trust of people who called him "reliable" and "trustworthy." He began his mission after the establishment of such an identity.

People knew his beautiful character, goodness and integrity prior to his prophethood and they loved him. His people, who gave him the nickname al-Amin (the Trustworthy), submitted to his judgement without objection when they fell in disagreement on returning the Black Stone to its place during the renovation of the Ka'bah.

Indeed, the Prophet (peace be upon him) strictly stood away from all kinds of wrong doing and from violating the rights of others. The only group he joined before his prophethood was Hilf al-Fudul, the Pact of the Virtuous. This was because Hilf al-Fudul was a group dedicated to serve justice, and the essence of its decisions was as follows:

"If the rights of a person from Mecca or abroad are violated, the wrong doer will be resisted immediately, standing on the side of the victim, until the harm is compensated. The distribution of rights and justice, peace and harmony of society will be ensured."

This pact against oppression and violation of rights attracted Rasulullah (peace be upon him) so much that he said after he became a Prophet:

"I was present in the house of Abdullah ibn Jud'an along with my uncles. I would not be more happy if I were to be given in its place red camels (meaning this worldly wealth). I would join such a group even if I was invited today." [8]

This and other endless examples of the manifestation of justice, mercy, and compassion in the life of the Prophet (peace be upon him) are examples for all humanity to emulate until the end of time. As a fair eye which discerns a bright light, this unattainable candle shining over the world cannot be denied its truth at least in the inner world. As a matter of fact, through rational evaluation, many non-Muslim scholars sincerely accepted his virtue and achievement. One of them, Thomas Carlyle, as pointed out before stated in his book *On Heroes, Hero-Worship and the Heroic in History* [9] that his birth reflected the emergence of light from darkness.

---

(8) Ibn Sa'd, *al-Tabakât*, I, 129; Ibn Hishâm, *al-Sirah al-Nabawiyyahh*, I, 133-134; Ahmad ibn Hanbal, *al-Musnad*, I, 190-193; al-Bayhaqî, *al-Sunan al-Kubrâ*, VI, 367.

(9) See page 50.

The Encyclopedia of Britannica, also, confirmed his virtue by declaring that at no time has a prophet or religious reformer reached the level of success that Muhammad (peace be upon him) reached.

Author Stanley Lane-Polo, truly confesses that the day Muhammad (peace be upon him) triumphed over his enemies was the same day he won the greatest battle of virtue over himself, as he freely forgave all the Qurayshites and extended his forgiveness to all Meccans.

Likewise, the author Arthur Gilman has observed his greatness during the conquering of Mecca. He said that the weight of what he had been put through by the Meccans could have easily led him to take revenge. Yet, he prohibited any kind of bloodshed by his army. He showed great mercy and remained grateful to Allah.

The Prophet as Perceived by the Polytheists

Prophet Muhammad (peace be upon him) gained the trust of polytheist Arabs during the period of Religious Ignorance (al-Jahliyya). Even Abu Jahl, the fiercest enemy of Islam, once said to him: "O Muhammad! I don't call you a liar, but I do not like the religion you brought..." [10].

His fiercest opponents accepted the trustworthiness of the Prophet (peace be upon him) in their hearts, but externally, they rejected him solely because of their arrogance. The Qur'an illustrates this as follows:

"We know indeed the grief which their words do cause thee: It

---

(10) Tirmidhî, *Tafsîr Sûrah 6*, 1; al-Hâkim, *al-Mustadrak*, II, 345.

is not thee they reject; it is the signs of Allah which the wicked deny" (Qur'an, An'am, 6/33).

❀

Heraclius, the Byzantine emperor of the time, who defeated the Persians in 628 AC, received a letter from the Prophet, while he was in Syria. The letter invited him to Islam. Heraclius showed interest in the letter instead of anger. He wanted to inquire and to gather more information about this new religion. For this purpose, he ordered that some countrymen of the new Prophet (peace be upon him) be brought before him. At that time, Abu Sufyan, who was a merciless enemy of the Prophet, was in Syria leading a caravan of Meccan merchants. It was the sixth year of Hijrah and there was a truce between polytheist Meccans and the Prophet. The men of Heraclius, who were in search of some Meccans who could provide them with information about the new Prophet, came across Abu Sufyan and his friends and took them to the emperor.

Heraclius and his circle were at the time in Ilya or Bayt al-Maqdis. Heraclius, accompanied by Greek leaders, accepted them in his presence and talked to them through an interpreter. Heraclius asked:

– Who is the closest relative of this person who proclaimed prophethood?

Abu Sufyan said:

– I am his closest relative here.

Heraclius ordered:

– Bring him and his friends closer! Let his friends stay

near to him while I talk to him.

He turned to his interpreter and said:

– Tell them that I will ask this man some questions about the new Prophet. If he lies they should warn me that he is lying.

When he was relating this story, Abu Sufyan said "By God, if I had not known that my friends would expose my lies, I would have certainly lied about him." Abu Sufyan narrated his dialogue with Heraclius as follows:

The first question Heraclius asked was:

– How is his lineage?

I said:

– His lineage is highly respected amongst us!

– Did anyone among you make similar claims before him?

– No, I said.

He asked:

– Was there a king among his parents and grandparents?

I said:

– No.

He asked:

– Are his followers from the lower or upper classes of people?

I answered:

– From the lower classes of people.

He asked:

– Does the number of his followers increase or decrease?

I replied:

– Their number increases.

He asked:

– Is there anyone among them who left the new religion because he disliked it?

I said:

– No.

He asked:

– Did you ever accuse him of lying before this incident?

I said:

– No.

He queried further:

– Did he ever break his promise?

I said:

– No, he keeps his promises but we made a truce with him for a certain time and do not know yet what he is going to do.

(Abu Sufyan said "this is the only thing I could include in my answers to potentially discredit him.)

Heraclius asked:

– Did you engage in wars with him?

I said:

– Yes.

Heraclius asked:

– How were the results of these wars?

I said:

– Sometimes we triumphed over him, sometimes he triumphed over us.

He asked:

– What are the things he commands you to do?

I replied:

– He requires us to worship one God alone, not to associate partners with him and to leave the idols our ancestors worshipped. He orders us to make salat, to be honest and chaste, to protect our honor and to maintain close and good relations with relatives.

Then Heraclius said to the interpreter:

– Tell him that I asked about his lineage. He said that it is highly respected amongst them. Prophets come from a respected lineage in their society.

I asked if there was anyone who made similar claims, he said no. If there was anyone before him like that I would have suspected that he was taking him as an example.

I asked whether there was a king among his ancestors; you said no. If it was so, I would have suspected that he was trying to regain his crown.

I asked if he had ever caught him lying before he made the claim to prophethood, he said, no. I am aware that one who does not lie to people does not lie about God either.

I queried about his followers whether they belonged to the upper or the lower classes in the society. He said they belonged to the lower ranks of their society. It is well-known that at the outset, the followers of the Prophets come from the lower ranks of society.

I wanted to know if the number of followers was increasing or decreasing. He said that they were increasing. One of the characteristics of a true religion is that their followers increase in the beginning.

I asked whether there was anyone who left this new religion after he had accepted it. He said no. This is what happiness is when the joy of faith enters the heart and grows roots in it.

I asked if he ever broke his promise; he said no. Prophets are like that; they never break their promises.

I asked about what he requires his followers to do. You said that he commands them to worship the one God, to not associate partners with him, in addition he requires them to perform ritual prayer, to be honest, and to be chaste and to lead an honorable life.

If what he has said is true, this person, will soon dominate even the land on which I now stand. I have already known about the emergence of such a Prophet, but I have not known that he would emerge from amongst you. If I knew that I could go to his presence, I would readily accept to face all the difficulties. If I were with him, I would wash his feet.

Then Heraclius asked for the letter which was had been brought to him by the messenger, Dihya. The letter was brought and read to him. The following was written in the letter:

"In the name of Allah, the Most Merciful and the Most Compassionate.

From Muhammad, the servant and messenger of Allah, to Heraclius, the leader of the Greek people.

Peace be on those who follow the right path.

I invite you to Islam. Embrace Islam, you will reach salvation and God will reward you twice. But if you refuse, you will be held responsible for your subjects as well.

"O People of the book! Come to common terms as between us and you that we worship none but Allah; that we associate no partners with Him; that we erect not from among you ourselves, Lords and patrons other than Allah." (Qur'an, Ali Imran, 3/64)"

Abu Sufyan said:

– After Heraclius had said what he said and after the reading of the letter was completed, a noise was heard and voices were raised in the group. As a result, they took us out. I said to my friends:

– Mohammed's work is growing. Even the kings have begun to listen to his message. Look at this, even the king of Bani Asfar (Greeks) is afraid of him!... Since then I retained the certainty that one day he would be successful. Eventually, Allah blessed me also with Islam [11]

❀

In our opinion, the objective attitude of the Byzantine emperor, Heraclius, towards what he heard, did not only come from his personal virtue.

The corruption of Christianity, which was originally a true religion and therefore based on faith in the unity of God, was at that time a new phenomenon. The fight over icons, which had lasted two centuries, had just ended and churches

---

(11) Bukhârî, *Jihâd* 102; Muslim, *Jihâd* 74.

were filled with pictures and statutes. Christianity fell from faith in the unity of God, and completely surrendered to the doctrine of the trinity. As a natural outcome of the corruption of such a revealed faith, Islam was sent to renew the "true faith". In spite of the degradation of their time, it is true that there were some people who maintained their faith in the unity of God. For instance, the emigrants who fled to Abyssinia because of the unbearable oppression in Mecca, met there King Najashi, who was similarly rightly guided. He even drew a line on the ground with his staff and said:

– The difference between my faith and what you are describing is less than this line.

King Najashi belonged to the sect of Arians which preserved the original creed of early Christianity. It is quite possible that Heraclius also carried such a faith. Yet there is no evidence that he accepted Islam. It should be mentioned once more that faith is a matter of divine blessing.

On the other hand, this incident demonstrates that even those who did not accept his message acknowledged the honesty and the perfect character of the Prophet. Before the immigration to Medina, commonly known as the Hijra, he was entrusted with some valuables by polytheists in Mecca to keep for them. As he decided to secretly leave Mecca, he assigned Ali to return them to their owners in Mecca on his behalf.

❀

The poet Kemal Edip Kurkcuoglu gives advice and warns the heedless who are removed from following the beautiful characteristics of the Prophet–only a small number of which have been described above.

Falling from the eye of the heart, alas! alas!
Is sufficient resentment in this world and the hereafter
for the spiritually unaware!

May Allah make us among his followers who obey him with love and reflect his qualities. He was an horizon of mercy and compassion, even the basic level of which is beyond reach.

He was working for the guidance of people with utmost sincerity. Yet they were cursing and stoning him. In response, he was praying for them. Zayd ibn Haritha, who was surprised by this, asked him:

– O the Messenger of Allah! They subject you to torture... but you still pray for them.

He said:

– What else can I do? I am sent for mercy, not for wrath... [12]

Does this not bear witness that he was at the zenith of giving, loyalty, good heartedness, mercy and compassion.

Humans who saw Krishna and Buddha as gods, Jesus as the son of God, and Pharaoh and Nimrod as lords, as well as those miserable people who worshiped animals, or such natural forces as fire, water and air, would have gladly accepted him as their "god". Yet, he proclaimed that *"As you, I am but a man. However, the inspiration has come to me that your Allah is the one Allah..."* (Qur'an, Kahf, 18/110).

---

(12) Muslim, *Birr* 87; Abû Ya'lâ, *al-Musnad*, XI, 35.

He added the word "abduhu," meaning his servant, at the beginning of the sentence (shahadah) uttered to announce acceptance of his prophethood because he wanted to ensure that his Community does not go astray.

The Messenger of Allah (peace be upon him) had always made clear that he had no superior powers. For instance, he said once:

– No one can enter Paradise only as a reward of his deeds.

Everyone was surprised. They asked:

– Even you, O the Messenger of Allah?

He said:

– Yes including me...! Unless the generosity of my Lord comes to my help! (Unless His blessing, mercy and forgiveness cover me, I will not be allowed to go to Paradise; my deeds would not be sufficient to save me...!) [13].

This system of principles is a divine grace which cannot be replicated by humanity.

This message is very refined, miraculous, filled with honesty and loyalty. Grasping the true meaning of the Qur'an and Sunnah is possible only through getting close to the depth of the heart and manners of the Prophet (peace be upon him).

No sentient being could successfully describe his real attributes. His high character and existence could not be comprehended. Scholars, philosophers, sultans of the heart, even the Archangel Gabriel considered being close to him the greatest honor and source of happiness for themselves.

---

(13) Bukhârî, *Rıqaq* 18; Muslim, *Munafiqun* 71-72; Ibn Mâjah, *Zuhd* 20 Dârimî, *Riqâq* 24; Ahmad ibn Hanbal, *al-Musnad*, II, 235.

The missions of all prophets were limited in time and space except for that of Prophet Muhammad (peace be upon him) who has been charged by Allah to be the Universal Guide of Humanity. Although a rich system of manners was not transmitted from the previous prophets to us, the mission of Prophet Muhammad (peace be upon him) was to encompass all times and places from the first revelation to the last day, and as a consequence Allah guaranteed that his manners including the smallest details were transmitted to us through reliable chains of narrators. This transmission has the potential of surviving until the last day. The reason behind this is the divine will to ensure that all people living in the last times can take him as the best role model (*uswa hasanah*).

Arabs customarily pledged on what they valued most. Although Allah has never done so for any other Prophet, He pledged in the Qur'an on the life of the Prophet (pbuh): "La a'mruk!" The Ottoman poet Shaikh Ghalib reiterated this pledge as follows:

O my leader! You are the sultan of prophets, you are the glorious king.

O my leader! You are the eternal source of joy for the helpless.

O my leader! You are the head of humanity in the divine presence.

O my leader! You are supported by Allah's pledge on your life, "la a'mruk!"

O my leader! You are Ahmad, Mahmud and Muhammad!

O my leader! You are the chosen sultan from Allah to us.

Another characteristic of the glorious Prophet (peace be upon him) is that he is addressed by Allah in the Qur'an as "O Nabi!", "O Rasul!", "O Mudhammil!", "O Muddathir!", but not with his proper name. Yet, other prophets were addressed by their proper names such as "O Adam!", "O Noah!", "O Abraham!", "O Moses!", "O David!", "O Jesus!", "O Zakariyya!", "O John!". In this distinction, we gain yet another measure of the uniqueness of the Prophet (peace be upon him).

Never forget to greet and salute him by salawat and salam! You will need his intercession (shafaah) and mediation on the most frightening day, that is the day of reckoning.

THE CHARACTER TRAITS
OF THE
PROPHET OF MERCY

"O Lord! Grant ease in my work rather than hardship and bring it to a blessed conclusion."   **(A classical prayer)**

In all of history, the only prophet and person whose life has been recorded in minute detail is Muhammad Mustafa (peace be upon him). His actions, words and feelings have been entirely recorded and they have taken their places as respected historical facts.

His life will be an example for generations to come, continuing up until the last day. In the Surah al-Qalam in the Qur'an, it is said about him: *"And thou (standest) on an exalted standard of character."* (Qur'an, Qalam, 68/4)

He was not only a teacher who was teaching the Qur'an verbally but at the same time, he was a living example who was practicing the Qur'an. Jabir narrates that Prophet Muhammad (peace be upon him) said:

"Allah, the Most High, sent me to perfect good morality" [1]

When he met the Prophet (peace be upon him), Abdullah ibn Salam, a former Jewish scholar who had converted to Islam, was overwhelmed by the light and the deep meaning he felt in his face. Impressed, he said:

---

(1) Muwatta, *Husn al-khuluq* 8; al-Bayhaqî, *al-Sunan al-Kubrâ*, X, 191; al-Qudâî, *Musnad al-Shihâb*, II, 192; al-Tabarânî, *al-Mu'jam al-Awsat*, VII, 74.

"A person who has such a face cannot be a liar". [2]

With that awareness, he embraced Islam.

Purity of Soul in the Prophet of Mercy

As mentioned earlier, the Prophet (peace be upon him) is a divine gift and a perfect example for the entirety of humanity. Everyone who is looking for happiness may follow his example to the extent he or she can. Each and every deed of the Prophet (peace be upon him) is a practical example for those who truly want to live Islam. Furthermore, there are some points that must be taken into consideration relative to benefits from the Essence of Muhammad:

1. Some deeds can be performed only by a power unique to the prophets. Others cannot imitate them regarding these points. As a matter of fact, even the Prophet (peace be upon him) warned the people around him about this issue. For instance, he frequently prayed at nights until his feet were swollen; and he fasted for days without a break.

2. Some of the deeds of the Prophet (peace be upon him) were especially for him alone: for instance, marrying more than four wives and prohibiting the receipt of charity either for himself or his progeny until the last day.

There is a great lesson to be learned in his immediate distribution of his share from the booties. He was careful about this his entire life up until his last breath:

---

(2) Tirmidhî, *Qıyâmah* 42; Ibn Mâjah, *Iqâmah* 174; Dârimî, *Salât* 156; Ahmad ibn Hanbal, *al-Musnad*, V, 451.

The Messenger of Allah (peace be upon him) was extremely ill and the time for his union with his Lord was approaching. Once he turned to his wife Aishah (may Allah be pleased with her) and asked her to distribute to the needy the 6-7 dinar which were with him. After a while he asked about the dinars. When he learned that Aishah forgot to give them out as charity because she was busy with his illness, he asked for the dinars, took them in his hand and said:

"Muhammad, the Messenger of Allah, does not expect to meet his Lord without distributing these to the needy..."

Then he gave them to five needy families of the Helpers (Ansar) in Medina. He said:

– Now I feel comfortable.[3]

Afterwards, he began a light sleep.

Ubaydullah ibn Abbas narrates the following:

One day, Abu Dharr told me:

– O my nephew! I will tell you a story.

Then he told me the following story:

Once I was with the Messenger of Allah (peace be upon him) He held my hand and said:

– O Abu Dharr! If the mountain of Uhud were to be turned into gold for me, I would spend it on the path of Allah and I would dislike to leave even a *qirat* [4] of it when I die.

I said:

---

(3) Ahmad b. Hanbal, *al-Musnad*, VI, 49, 86, 182; Ibn Hibbân, *al-Sahîh*, II, 491; al-Humaydî, *al-Musnad*, I, 135.

(4) The smallest measure of weight, like a gram today. A qirat was equal to five barley beans.

– O the Messenger of Allah! Is it a *qirat* or a *qantar* [5] that you would not like to leave behind.

He said:

– O Abu Dharr! I am decreasing, you are increasing. I want the Hereafter, you want this world! I would not leave even a *qirat*, a *qirat*, a *qirat*.

He repeated the word *qirat* three times in his answer [6]

The sublime state of the Messenger of Allah (peace be upon him) represents the highest criterion. Those who are required to follow it are not obliged to reach to that level. Consequently, it would be problematic if the Muslim community attempted to follow each example in an exact and strict manner. Regardless, it is beyond human power. The wisdom behind this concerns only the Prophet.

The deeds emanating from a reason related exclusively to the person of the Prophet are not limited only to the above mentioned examples. Another example is the regulations concerning distribution of his material legacy. This is also exclusive to him and does not constitute an example for others to follow.

He said "we are the prophet, we do not leave material legacy" [7] and he distributed everything he owned. This was not meant to serve as a rule for others to follow.

---

(5) Another measure of weight. If we take *qirat* as analogous to a gram, we can take *qintar* as analogous to a kilogram.

(6) Bukhârî, *Buyû* 100; Muslim, *Zakât* 31; Abû Dâwûd, *Vitr* 23; Dârimî, *Riqâq* 53; Ahmad ibn Hanbal, *al-Musnad*, II, 467.

(7) Bukhârî, *Khumus* 1; Muslim, *Jihâd* 54; Abû Dâwûd, *Imârah* 19; Tirmidhî, *Siyar* 44; Nasâî, *Fay'* 9; Muwatta, *Kalâm* 27; Ahmad ibn Hanbal, *al-Musnad*, I, 4.

Likewise, it is known that the Prophet (peace be upon him) said, "The gift for a believer in this world is poverty" [8]. He was proud of his poverty. This attitude is also due to a reason exclusively related to his person. It should not be thought that he was encouraging poverty. On the contrary, he also said that "the hand which gives is better than the hand which receives"[9]. In this principle, it can be said, he was encouraging one to gain wealth through legal means with the purpose of becoming someone who can give.

For this reason, the regulations about poverty are not to encourage poverty, but to encourage one to be content with the divine plan as well as to rely on and submit to the will of Allah.

3. Living in accordance with the principles of *Zuhd* (divorcing the heart from this world) and *Taqwa* (staying away from doubtful issues) is a virtue of great character which brings one closer to Allah. Yet, not all members of a society can be forced to lead such a life because it depends on inherent ability and talent. In so far as all social systems explicitly and implicitly encourage cultural growth, there is no necessary conflict between cultural dynamism and spiritual integrity. Consequently, although zuhd and taqwa deny the pleasures of this world, adherence to them on a communal level need not lead to a deterioration in social dynamism where spiritually rich communities would thus be superseded by their more worldly enemies. It is a general rule

(8) al-Daylamî, *al-Firdaws*, II, 70.
(9) Bukhârî, *Vasâyâ* 9; Muslim, *Zakât* 94; Abû Dâwûd, *Zakât* 28; Tirmidhî, *Zuhd* 32; Nasâî, *Zakât* 50; Muwatta, *Sadakah* 8; Dârimî, *Zakât* 22; Ahmad ibn Hanbal, *al-Musnad*, II, 67.

that we must measure our progress on a daily basis, as is expressed in the hadith which states that "the one whose two days remain equal to each other is not from us"[10]. Here we see proof of the fact that this rule does not fall in contradiction with the principles of *zuhd* and *taqwa* which are based on disinterest in mundane pleasures. This is because disinterest in the mundane life is not on the level of practical existence and appearance but rather on a spiritual and mental level.

As Jalaladdin Rumi, (may Allah keep his soul pure), said:

"The meaning of the mundane (dunya) is unawareness of divine presence! It is not about money, women, dress. Understand this well."[11]

From this perspective, owning property and being wealthy does not contradict zuhd and taqwa as long as one does not become a spend thrift and give them a place in the heart. On the other hand, little wealth and money may become idols if love of them enters the heart. From the prophets, the life of Suleiman (peace be upon him) and from the companions, the lives of Abu Bakr, Uthman, Talha and Abd ar-Rahman ibn Awf, may Allah be pleased with them all, are excellent examples of this balance.

Occasionally, some of the appearances of taqwa and zuhd may be due to material necessity rather than a deep disinterest in this world. In such cases, taqwa would be accepting poverty with joy in what was predestined by Allah.

---

(10) al-Bayhaqî, *Kitâb al-Zuhd al-kabîr*, II, 367; al-Daylamî, *al-Firdaws*, III 611; Abû Nu'aym al-Isbahânî, *Hilyah al-Awliyâ*, VIII, 35.

(11) Can Şefik, *Mesnevi Tercemesi*, (Istanbul, 1997), v. II, p. 55.

However, if instead of accepting it that way, one merely denied the existence of his true circumstance, it would be a misinterpretation of taqwa. For instance, although Rasulullah sometimes tied a stone to his belly to suppress the feeling of inescapable hunger, his example reveals that the best way of thanksgiving is to share freely with others. This is the most fitting form of *sobriety* (taqwa) and *abstention* (zuhd). Hiding one's wealth and feigning stinginess as piety is a form of deception and thus can never be true.

Examined according to the measures of this perspective, it can be seen that he was the most pious of human beings. He was living as the poor because of his taqwa. Aishah (may Allah be pleased with her) said:

"Prophet Muhammad passed away without filling his stomach for two consecutive days with barley bread."[12]

Anas (may Allah be pleased with him) narrated that:

"There were times when Rasulullah (peace be upon him) accepted invitations to meals consisting of barley bread and fat on the verge of spoiling. In his humility, he freely attended such gatherings. Moreover, he put his shield in pawn to a Jew. But because of his donations and gifts, he was unable to redeem it." [13]

Nevertheless, the Prophet (peace be upon him) prohibited self-deprivation from halal food and drinks on the grounds of piety. He ate and drank what was halal. Yet, at the

---

(12) Bukhârî, *Aymân*, 22; Muslim, *Zuhd* 20-25; Nasâî, *Dahâyâ* 37; Ibn Mâjah, *At'imah*, 48; Ahmad ibn Hanbal, *al-Musnad*, II, 98.

(13) Buhkari, *Jihâd* 89; Tirmidhî, *Buyû* 7; Nasâî, *Buyû* 58; Ibn Mâjah, *Ruhûn* 1; Dârimî, *Buyû* 44; Ahmad ibn Hanbal, *al-Musnad*, I, 236.

same time, he did not fill his stomach because the food was halal. Furthermore, he said to a man who belched in his presence:

– Stop belching! Those who fill their stomachs excessively in this world are the ones who will suffer hunger longer." [14]

Another hadith states that:

"No one has filled a container more risky than his stomach. Indeed, a few bites is sufficient for a person to keep himself standing. If he has to eat more, he should reserve one third for food, one third for drink and one third for easy breathing." [15]

This is the middle way in eating and drinking.

This constitutes a system of extraordinary measures aimed at controlling greed in human beings. From this perspective, the school of the Prophet (peace be upon him) educated the poor and the rich alike including statesmen from different ranks of society in the best way, with the best content, and their hearts gained happiness to the extent that they obeyed him. In this prophetic school, there were many rich people who lived humbly as if they were poor, and, many poor people who lived gratefully before Allah as if they were rich. Many wealthy people and statesmen who worked continuously for charity were educated in that school. In Islamic history, the stories of caliphs who carried food on their backs to the poor, and cooked meals for them

---

(14) Tirmidhî, *Sifatu'l-qiyâmah* 37; Ibn Mâjah, *At'imah* 50; al-Tabarânî, *al-Mu'jam al-Awsat*, IV, 249; al-Bayhaqî, *Shu'ab al-Îmân*, V, 27.

(15) Tirmidhî, Zuhd 47; Ibn Mâjah, *At'imah* 50; Ahmad ibn Hanbal, *al-Musnad*, IV, 132; al-Hâkim, *al-Mustadrak*, IV, 135; Ibn Hibbân, *al-Sahîh*, II, 449.

are well-known [16]. The trial of Fatih Sultan Muhammad arising from a complaint by a Greek architect and his respect for the court's decision in favor of dhimmis (non-Muslim subjects of the state) is just one of the manifestations of blessings and mercy for humanity arising from the Prophet's school of taqwa.

The Messenger of Allah (peace be upon him) defined zuhd in an excellent way:

"Zuhd towards this world is not making haram what is halal, nor is it abandoning wealth. But Zuhd towards this world is reliance on what is in the hand of Allah more than relying on what is in your hand and during the time of affliction is to hope for the reward of endurance" [17]. In his zuhd and contentment, Rasulullah (peace be upon him) is eternally the best example for all of humanity. Zuhd is what brings a splendid life and happiness to one's heart and body by controlling excessive desires towards mundane pleasures, by not being deceived by transient worldly joys, by not letting this world occupy one's heart, by not loving things other than Allah and his Prophet, abandoning what takes away from worship and gives no benefit in the Hereafter. Conversely, loving this world is a disaster full of pain and anxiety which exhausts the energy of the heart and the body. Prophet Muhammad (peace be upon him) said:

"Zuhd towards this world brings comfort to heart and body. Love of the world increases sorrow and pain..." [18]

(16) Suyûtî, *Tarikh al-khulefâ*, p. 91-92.

(17) Tirmidhî, *Zuhd* 29; Ibn Mâjah, *Zuhd* 1 ; al-Tabarânî, *al-Mu'jam al-Awsat*, VIII, 57; al-Bayhaqî, *Shu'ab al-Îmân*, VII, 218.

(18) Ahmad ibn Hanbal, *Kitâb al-Zuhd*, p. 47; al-Qudâî, *Musnad al-Shihâb*, I,

Another hadith expresses the following advice:

"Show disinterest towards this world and Allah will like you; show disinterest in what is in the hands of people and people will like you!..." [19]

Zuhd comes first among the measures recommended to take against the dangers of this world. A hadith states that:

"White is not superior over black. No race is superior over another. Superiority is only by taqwa."[20]

He also said:

"The revelation did not command me to accumulate wealth, nor to become a merchant. It was revealed to me "to spread the glory of your Lord, to be among those who prostrate to Allah and serve him." [21]

Another hadith gives the following advice:

"When you stand for salat, pray as if it is your last salat. Do not say what you will resent tomorrow. Do not desire what people heedlessly desire" [22]

Once he was asked:

188; al-Bayhaqî, *Shu'ab al-Îmân*, VII, 368 [Narrated also from Omar as *mawkuf hadith*].

(19) Ibn Mâjah, *Zuhd* 1; al-Hâkim, *al-Mustadrak*, IV, 348 ; al-Tabarânî, *al-Mu'jam al-Kabîr*,VI, 193; al-Bayhaqî, *Shu'ab al-Îmân*, VII, 344.

(20) Ahmad ibn Hanbal, *al-Musnad*, V, 158; al-Bayhaqî, *Shu'ab al-Îmân*, IV, 289.

(21) Ibn Abî 'Âsım, *Kitâb al-Zuhd*, I, 391; al-Daylamî, *al-Firdaws*, IV, 95; Abû Nu'aym al-Isbahânî, *Hilyah al-Awliyâ*, II, 131; Ibn 'Adiyy, *al-Kâmil fî al-du'afâ*, III, 68.

(22) Ahmad ibn Hanbal, *al-Musnad*, V, 412; Ibn Mâjah, *Zuhd* 15; al-Tabarânî, *al-Mu'jam al-Kabîr*, IV, 154.

"Who is the most perfect human?"

He replied:

"The pure ones are those who clean themselves from sin, doubt, cheating, lying and jealousy" [23]

Prophet Muhammad was very careful about halal and haram. He also stood away from doubtful matters. Once, his grandson, Hasan, who was at that time a small child, was sitting in his grandfather's lap in the masjid and watching how the dates for zakat were distributed. Suddenly he put one of the dates in his mouth, Rasulullah (peace be upon him) immediately warned him:

"Throw it away! Throw it away! Throw the date away! Do you not know we do not eat charity?" He made his young grandchild to throw the date from his mouth to the floor" [24]

Mawlana Jalaluddin Rumi, (may Allah keep his soul pure), says about halal food:

"Bites are like seeds. Their fruit is thought, ideas and intentions."

"The food that brings you greater desire and motivation for, and pleasure from, worship and submission is halal; and the food that brings you laziness towards worship and submission to Allah and hardens your heart is haram."

"Increase the number of halal bites in your life! Stay

---

(23) Ibn Hibbân, *al-Sahîh*, II, 76; Ibn Abî Shaybah, *al-Musannaf*, VI, 167; Ma'mar ibn Râshid, *al-Jâmi'*, XI, 191.

(24) Bukhârî, *Zakât* 60; Muslim, *Zakât* 161; Nasâî, *Tahârah* 105; Muwatta, *Sadakah* 13; Ahmad ibn Hanbal, *al-Musnad*, I, 200.

away from haram and doubtful bites so that you can get the taste of worship and obedience to Allah and reach contentment and concentration of heart" [25]

Allah the Most High says in the Qur'an:

"Successful indeed are the believers who are humble in their prayers," (Qur'an, Mu'minun, 23/1-2).

❊

The prevailing view in our society is that religion is a system of beliefs whose only aim is to bring happiness in the Hereafter. Yet, religion is not an institution with the sole purpose of acquiring happiness in the Hereafter; it also aims to create an environment of tranquility and security for humans by bringing order to social life.

One night, Umar, may Allah be pleased with him, was as usual walking the streets of Medina. Suddenly, he stopped because he unintentionally overheard the conversation between a mother and a daughter. The conversation drew his attention. The mother was saying to her daughter:

– Put some water in the milk, which we will sell tomorrow.

The daughter was saying:

– Mother! Have not you heard that the Caliph prohibited putting water in the milk.

The mom got angry and raised her voice:

– Daughter! How do you think the Caliph will know at this hour of the night that we put water in the milk?

(25) Rûmî, Jalâladdin, *Mathnawî Ma'nawî*, (Tehran, 1378) v.I, 1645-48; Can Şefik, *Mesnevi Tercemesi*, (Istanbul, 1997), v.II, p.120.

The daughter whose heart was alive with respect to God, could not easily accept the cheating her mother proposed by adding water to the milk. She continued to object:

– Mother! Let us accept that the Caliph does not see, how about Allah? Do you think He does not see either? It is easy to hide this cheating from people, but it is impossible to hide it from Allah who sees and hears everything.

The answers which the girl, whose heart was full of divine knowledge, gave to her mother, out of a deeper respect and fear of Allah, touched the heart of Umar, may Allah be pleased with him. Amir al-Mu'minin, the Leader of the Believers, realized that although she was an ordinary girl; she had an exceptional God-consciousness. He wanted her to be his daughter in law and married her to his son. From this pure chain came Umar ibn Abdulaziz who is considered the fifth rightly guided caliph.

This incident demonstrates that respecting the borders of halal is sufficient to bring happiness and elevate humans to the level of perfection. In contrast, showing discontent with the endless halal boundaries created by Allah and getting involved in what is haram or doubtful are not appropriate for a servant. Prophet Muhammad (peace be upon him) said about doubtful matters, which are not clearly discernable whether they are haram or not:

"Leave what gives doubt to your heart and adopt what has no doubt in it" [26]

Yet, it would not be correct either to misinterpret the

---

(26) Bukhârî, *Buyû* 3; Tirmidhî, *Qıyâmah* 60; Ahmad ibn Hanbal, *al-Musnad*, III, 153.

principle by going to the strange extreme of staying away even from halal things, or by creating confusion about halal matters.

Islam requires balance and following the middle way in this issue as it does in all issues. The purpose of Islam is not to impose limits on humans; on the contrary, its goal is to make them live in tranquility, happiness and stability. The secret of this is achieved by restoring the place of the heart. This is because all beauty springs from the essence of the heart. It becomes possible by hearing, feeling and applying the deep and refined attributes of the heart of the Prophet (peace be upon him).

❀

Prophet Muhammad (peace be upon him) had no sins. Yet he continued to pray at night until his feet were swollen and he continued to recite the Qur'an until he got exhausted. He loved, thanked, feared and remembered Allah more than anyone else.

Salat is the union of the servant with his Lord. It is going up to the divine presence. It is a source of endless pleasure for the lovers of Allah. They make voluntary worship with the purpose of maintaining the pleasure of worship.

There is submission in the salat. This is the reason why the ego dislikes it. Only this characteristic is sufficient to show that Islam is a true religion and that salat is the highest form of worship.

Those who are overcome by their ego, do not come close to salat while those who cannot pass the obstacle of their ego stick to the form of salat. The real salat is a blessing given to only a few people.

The Messenger of Allah expressed this truth as follows:

"Two people may make salat in the same place but the difference between them is like the difference between the earth and the sky" [27].

❀

The fast of the Light of Existence is also an excellent example for his community, the Ummah.

He began fasting most of the time when he was hungry. Sometimes he fasted consecutive days without a meal at night. When his companions also wanted to do the same, he said to them:

– "You have no power to do it the way I do." [28].

Ibn Abbas, may Allah be pleased with him and his father, narrated that the Prophet (peace be upon him) used to spend a few consecutive nights hungry while his household, also, could not find anything to eat. Even when they ate, their meal was only barley bread [29].

Anas ibn Malik (may Allah be pleased with him) narrated that one day our Mother Fatimah brought some bread she cooked to the Prophet (peace be upon him). He asked:

– What is this?

Fatimah replied:

– A nice kind of bread I cooked, I could not eat without offering some to you.

(27) Abû Sa'îd al-Shâshî (d.335), *Musnad al-Shashî*, I, 86.
(28) Bukhârî, *Sawm* 20; Muslim, *Sıyâm* 55; Muwatta, *Sıyâm* 37; Ahmad ibn Hanbal, *al-Musnad*, II, 128.
(29) Ibn Sa'd, *al-Tabaqât al-Kubra*, I, 400.

The pride of the world said:

– This is the first bite your father will have had for the last three days.

According to Abu Hurayra, the Messenger of Allah (peace be upon him) at times, used to tie a stone to his belly to suppress the feeling of hunger [30].

The high value of fasting comes from its purpose, which is the struggle against "nafs" and controlling it with a continuous feeling of worship.

The pilgrimage is, on the other hand, to take a lesson in tawakkul, the reliance on God of Abraham and Ishmael (peace be on them), to stone the internal enemy, which is called "nafs" and the external enemy, which is called "shaytan," to leave behind all class differences by dressing in a shroud-like cloth and seeking refuge in the Creator, to be thrilled by feeling the frightful scene of the day of resurrection, to bring together foreign communities of Muslims from afar, and to establish a brotherhood of faith.

What an excellent example is the Farewell Pilgrimage and Sermon of the Prophet (peace be upon him) for the pilgrimages his community will make up until the last day!

In his Last Sermon, the Prophet (peace be upon him) made at the same time a "distribution of love." The major lines of the rights between Muslims were outlined by "the cement of love."

The rituals of the pilgrimage turn one's eyes to the spiritual life because this refined worship is full of

(30) Ibn Sa'd, *al-Tabaqât al-Kubra*, I, 400.

manifestations of love, which is tender and merciful, such as the prohibition of hunting, of picking a green leaf or of hurting a creature of Allah.

Umar, may Allah be pleased with him, gave up kissing the Black Stone, al-Hagar al-Aswad, out of concern for disturbing other Muslims.

These deeds and states of mind during the pilgrimage bring one face to face with self-questioning and are reflected in the future lives of the people involved. The only goal of all these activities is to grow closer to Allah, the Most High.

The sacred places where the pilgrimage is performed are the spiritual environs of a sublime world.

Arafat is a place of forgiveness and refuge.

Muzdalifa is the place of the manifestation of mercy, which is pointed out in the Qur'an as al-Mash'ar al-Haram [31].

Mina is a place of submission to and reliance on Allah where Abraham, Ishmael, and our mother Hagar triumphed over Shaytan.

The Ka'bah is the direction faced for salat, which was ordered by Allah, the Most High, in the Qur'an: *"But prostrate thyself, and draw near (unto Allah)."* (Qur'an, Alaq, 96/19). At the same time, it is the point to which all Muslims around the world turn their face in salat; that is; it is the place where the pulse of the Muslim world is felt.

The City of the Prophet (peace be upon him) which we visit after Mecca, is a place where the heart reaches high levels after getting ornamented with the designs of love. The

---

(31) Qur'an, Baqara, 2/198.

Prophet (peace be upon him) is the only one who was addressed by Allah as "beloved".

According to Imam Malik, the place housing the grave of the Prophet is one of the most blessed places in the world after the Ka'bah. This is because he was the guide of all humanity.

This blessed land has been nourished by the spirituality of the faithful since the time of Adam and is watered by their tears. These places, which have been the fountains of the inspirations of the prophets, are full of invaluable memories in the history of the prophets.

Briefly put, the performance of Hajj is a comprehensive worship, which as an obligation leads a person to the perfection of religion.

Hajj is a worship through which one's soul regains tranquility, original climate, color and identity. It is full of spiritual manifestations where the heart gets cleaned and purified by the rain of spiritual blessings and reaches its truth.

❀

Zakat is a religious tax imposed on those who own enough to make it necessary for them to give to the needy. This is necessary to make the remaining wealth halal for the owner. Wealth is gradually transferred in parts to the needy in the society. This distribution of wealth allows for the establishment of social balance, justice and harmony.

What is taken into consideration in zakat is not one's annual income but a believer's accumulated wealth.

Consequently, the wealth which is not used in investment gradually vanishes. That means Islam provides a dynamism to society by mobilizing all the wealth from property and finance.

The wisdom behind zakat and charity is to provide an effective solution for the endless growth of personal wealth which may eventually become a chronic tumor.

Zakat is a means by which the relationship of sincerity and love grows between the one who gives zakat and the one who receives it. In other words, zakat is the right of the poor on the wealthy, which strengthens mutual love. In the Qur'an, this is described as follows:

"And in their wealth and possessions (was remembered) the right of the (needy,) him who asked, and him who (for some reason) was prevented (from asking)." (Qur'an, Zariyat, 51/19).

Adab (Islamic etiquette) is very important. The one who gives must feel thankful to the one who takes because the needy allow the rich to fulfill an obligatory worship and to gain a reward from Allah. Charity given for the sake of Allah is at the same time a shelter against illnesses and other troubles. The Qur'an draws our attention to the importance of giving zakat and charity by stating that, *"He receives their gifts of charity"* (Tawba, 104). Similarly, a hadith also declares that, "charity reaches first the hand of Allah, then the hand of the poor."[32]

When giving charity, it is essential to avoid arrogance, haughtiness, disdain and showing off. Otherwise, what is given would not reach to the hand of Allah but instead

---

(32) al-Tabarânî, *al-Mu'jam al-Kabîr*, IX, 109; al-Harawî, *al-Arba'în fî dalâil al-Tawhîd*, I, 74; al-Daylamî, *al-Firdaws*, II, 52.

would be wasted in the hands of transient beings and eventually nothing would reach to the Next World. Prophet Muhammad (peace be upon him) led an exemplary life with respect to abstention from worldly pleasures and with respect to giving out charity. Our Mother Aishah said:

"Two dishes never entered at the same time the stomach of the Messenger of Allah in one day. When he ate meat, he did not eat anything else. Likewise, when he ate dates or bread, he did not add anything to them." [33]

Abu Nadr narrates the following:

I heard that Our Mother Aishah said:

"One day we were sitting with the Messenger of Allah. My father, Abu Bakr, offered us a leg of lamb. In the darkness of the night, we were trying to cut the meat. One said: "Do you not have a candle or light?" I said: "If we had oil, we would have eaten it."[34]

Prophet Muhammad (peace be upon him) loved very much to give charity. Once he said to Bilal:

"O Bilal! Give charity! Do not be afraid that the owner of the Throne will decrease your wealth because of giving charity" [35].

Therefore, the Messenger of Allah (peace be upon him) was never interested in accumulating wealth. This was because he had made the intention to pass his life as a "servant prophet" as is explained in the following hadith:

---

(33) Ibn Sa'd, *al-Tabaqât al-Kubrâ*, I, 405.
(34) Ibn Sa'd, *al-Tabaqât al-Kubrâ*, I, 405.
(35) Ma'mar ibn Râshid, *al-Jâmi'*, XI, 108; al-Bazzâr, *al-Musnad*, IV, 204; al-Tabarânî, *al-Mu'jam al-Awsat*, III, 86; al-Bayhaqî, *Shabul-Îmân*, II, 118.

"I was given the choice between being a servant prophet or a king prophet. The Archangel hinted to me to keep myself humble. Therefore, I chose to be a servant prophet and expressed my wish "to be one day satiated and one day hungry" [36].

Prophet Muhammad (peace be upon him) refused to enter the house of his daughter Fatimah (may Allah be pleased with her) because she decorated her home, and he said to her:

"It would not be appropriate for us to enter decorated places" [37].

Yet, Prophet Muhammad (peace be upon him) did not praise himself because of the highly pious life he was leading. He used to count the blessings of Allah on him while showing extreme humility by saying "la fakhr" [38], "no pride".

The Humility of the Prophet of Mercy

Extreme praise and appreciation by others usually leads one to arrogance. These two situations corrupt and spoil most people. Although Rasulullah (peace be upon him) was the best of humanity and praised by Allah, he made the following request of his companions:

"Call me 'the servant and messenger of Allah'." [39]

---

(36) İbn Hibban, *al-Sahîh*, XIV, 280 ; al-Bayhaqî, *al-Sunan al-Kubrâ*, VII, 48, 49.

(37) Abû Dâwûd, *At'imah* 8; Ibn Mâjah, *At'imah* 56; Ahmad ibn Hanbal, *al-Musnad*, V, 220-222.

(38) Tirmidhî, *Manâqıb* 1; Ibn Mâjah, *Zuhd* 37; Ahmad ibn Hanbal, *al-Musnad*, I, 5, 281.

(39) Bukhârî, *Anbiyâ* 48; Dârimî, *Riqâq* 68; Ahmad ibn Hanbal, *al-Musnad*, I, 23.

Abu Usamah (may Allah be pleased with him) narrated that:

"The speech of the Prophet (peace be upon him) was derived from the Qur'an. He continuously made *dhikr* and kept his speeches short while keeping his *salat* long. He never felt ashamed of walking along with a poor or needy person in order to help that individual; on the contrary, he took pleasure from doing so." [40]

Anas (may Allah be pleased with him) narrated that:

"Rasulullah (peace be upon him) made dhikr very often. He joked very little. He rode a donkey, wore cloth made of rough wool, accepted the invitations of the slaves, visited the ill and attended funeral services. You should have seen him on the day the castle of Khaibar was conquered, when he was riding a donkey with a halter made of date leaves. The more God blessed him with triumph, the more humble and grateful he became." [41]

Jarir (may Allah be pleased with him) narrated the following:

"A man came into the presence of the Prophet (peace be upon him) on the day Mecca was conquered. The man started shaking as he saw the spiritual and physical grandeur of the Prophet, (peace be upon him). When the Prophet (peace be upon him) saw him in that position, he said to the man with a soft voice:

"Relax, do not feel distressed! I am not a king. I am the

---

(40) Nasâî, *Jum'a* 31; Dârimî, *Muqaddimah* 13; Ibn Hibbân, *al-Sahîh*, XIV, 333; al-Hâkim, *al-Mustadrak*, II, 671.
(41) Tirmidhî, *Janâiz* 32; Ibn Mâjah, *Zuhd* 16; al-Hâkim, *al-Mustadrak*, II, 506.

son of a woman from the tribe of Quraysh who used to eat sun-dried meat." [42]

Amir ibn Rabi'a (may Allah be pleased with him) narrated that:

"One day, I was going to the mosque with the Prophet. The lace of his shoe broke on the way. I wanted to take it to repair it. The Messenger of Allah refused to give it to me and said:

'This is self-preference (that is keeping oneself above others), I dislike self-preference'." [43]

The Messenger of Allah (peace be upon him) gave guidance to attain to eternal happiness for the entirety of humanity. This was as a gift from him, because he did not ask anything in return for the great service he provided to others.

❀

The purpose of religion is to raise good, refined humans, with deep understanding and feeling. This happens through developing a consciousness of the worship of Allah. This maturity is reached through the excitement that takes place in the heart as described in the following verse:

"For, Believers are those who, when Allah is mentioned, feel a tremor in their hearts, and when they hear His revelation rehearsed, find their faith strengthened, and put (all) their trust in their Lord" (Qur'an, Anfal, 8/2).

---

(42) Ibn Mâjah, *At'imah* 30 ; al-Hâkim, *al-Mustadrak,* II, 506; al-Tabarânî, *al-Mujamu l-Awsat,* II, 64.

(43) al-Bazzâr, *al-Musnad,* IX, 263; Abû Dâwûd al-Tayâlisî, *al-Musnad,* I, 156; al-Tabarânî, *al-Mu'jam al-Awsat,* III, 174; al-Bayhaqî, *Shu'ab al-Îmân,* III, 275.

The Arabic word for human is "insan" which is related to "nisyan" (forgetting) and "uns" (friendship). The opposite of "nisyan" is "dhikr" (remembrance), which is repeated in the Qur'an more than 250 times. If the essence of dhikr is established at the center of the heart, this heart begins to know and worship Allah. Lovers never forget their beloved. They always keep them in their hearts and in their tongues. The hearts which desire to enjoy a faithful life, maintain ceaseless dhikr. They are immersed in thoughts about the creation of the earth and the skies by Allah while they are walking, sitting or lying down as illustrated in the following Qur'anic verse:

"Men who remember Allah standing, sitting, and lying down on their sides, and contemplate the (wonders) of creation in the heavens and the earth, (by saying): 'Our Lord not for naught hast thou created (all) this! Glory to Thee! Give us salvation from the Chastisement of the Fire'" (Qur'an, Ali Imran, 3/191).

A heart without such depth and refinement would not desire Allah the Most High as described in the verse below:

"Woe to those whose hearts are hardened against the remembrance" (Qur'an, Zumar, 39/22). This verse indicates that the humans who fall away from dhikr lose the honor of being a human being.

Humans carry the quality of being a worshiper. So, they either worship material things and interests or their Lord. To worship the Lord protects humans from becoming slaves to personal interests and material things.

Allah, the Most High, warns against this in the following verse:

"Hast thou seen him who maketh his desire his god?" (Qur'an, Jathiya, 45/23).

Nourishing long term desires and plans in one's mind to be realized in the distant future, that belong exclusively to this world and not the next world, will lead one to a bitter end. The Prophet (peace be upon him) said:

"Be aware! Do not let your desires and future plans increase to such a degree that they make you forget your death! Otherwise your hearts gets hardened. ... Open your eyes! What is going to come is very near!" [(44)].

Salman al-Farisi who benefited greatly from the advise of the Prophet (peace be upon him) said: "Three things make me laugh while three things make me cry". He explained that one of the things that surprised him and made him laugh was the one who makes long term plans although death is awaiting him.

The Prophet (peace be upon him), also said: "Even though all the powers of an aged person weaken, his greed and desires concerning the distant future (tul al-amal) remain ever young" [(45)].

The above hadith illustrates that greed and desires for the distant future are two handicaps from which no human heart is saved. Even if bodies weaken and age, humans desire to remain young because their souls have the quality of immortality. Consequently, humans always want to

---

(44) Ibn Mâjah, *Muqaddimah* 7; Ma'mar ibn Râshid, *al-Jâmi'*, XI, 116; al-Qudâî, *Musnad al-Shihâb*, II, 263; al-Tabarânî, *al-Mu'jam al-Awsat*, VIII, 31.
(45) Bukhârî, *Riqâq* 5; Muslim, *Zakât* 114.

remain young and regret losing their youth as they get old. As a result, they are enslaved by an endless greed.

As is the case of dry earth soaking up the rainwater which falls on it, the human ego aims to absorb all worldly pleasures in itself. However, humans do not return the favor imparted by the rain as in the case of the earth which produces fruits. In their failure to return the fruit of charity their hearts are hardened for lack of integrity and slavery to earthly interests.

❀

The purpose of bad qualities in creation is to facilitate the testing of humans. For this reason, the verse below in the Qur'an states that: *"By the Soul, and the proportion and order given to it; and its inspiration as to its wrong and its rights; truly he succeeds that purifies it, and he fails that corrupts it"* (Qur'an, Shams, 91/7-10).

The high rank of humans, who are created with incomprehensible complexity and immeasurable depth, is realized by obeying Allah solely and spending their lives protecting their hearts from evil.

The raid of Tabuk was full of challenges. The companions traveled hundreds of kilometers and turned back home. As they approached Medina, even their appearance began to change because of hunger; their skin stuck to their bones, their hair and beard were unruly. Prophet Muhammad (peace be upon him) said: "Now, we are going from a small war to a big war!.." The companions asked with great surprise: "O the Messenger of Allah! Is there a war more difficult than the one we just had?" Prophet

Muhammad (peace be upon him) said: "Now we are returning to the Great War (the war against ego, nafs)..." [46].

The war against the ego is taught through the education and the training of the heart. The purpose of this war is to elevate morality and help humans to reach the level of perfection, *al-insan al-kamil*.

This secret can only be unveiled through the truth emanating from Muhammad (peace be upon him). If a human cannot discover the reason behind the creation of this world, it will swallow him. The one who is unaware of the reason he came to this world leads a life without knowing the sacred structure of humans. Nor will he comprehend the divine purpose in the creation of humanity. He will fail to comprehend what is being a vicegerent of Allah on earth. Yet those who strive to become a vicegerent of Allah on the earth will become the seeing eye of the Lord and his hearing ear [47]. Their aim in life is union with Allah.

❀

In this world, somethings may not be absolutely explained by the human intellect alone. Even our words of explanation need to be explained by other words. While trying to explain what is inexplicable by vague means, aren't we forgetting that the most inexplicable reality transcending the reach of the intellect is in fact Allah. Allah is the only and the absolute

---

(46) al-Bagdâdî, *Tarîkhu Bagdâd*, XIII, 523; [Some version of this hadith was narrated from İbRahîm ibn Abi 'Abla as *maktu hadıth*, See ; al-Mizzî, *Tahdhîb al-Kamâl*, II, 144; al-Zahabî, *Siyar a'lâm al-nubalâ*, VI, 325].

(47) Bukhârî, *Riqâq* 38; Ahmad ibn Hanbal, *al-Musnad*, VI, 256; İbn Hibban, *al-Sahîh*, II, 58; al-Bayhaqî, *al-Sunan al-Kubrâ*, III, 346.

explanation of this world. We can know him only to the extent that we gain love and wisdom, and only to the extent that we submit.

The intellect is limited. We can only have access beyond the limit of the intellect where the secrets of the world lie, through the heart. Abraham (peace be upon him) expressed this as follows. He said: *"I have surrendered to the Lord of the Worlds."* (Qur'an, Baqara, 2/131).

Imam Ghazzali related his experience concerning this question as follows: "I stretched my intellect to such an extent that it was about to break apart. I came to realize that it is limited. It alone cannot go to an ultimate point. I experienced a kind of insanity and I almost lost my mind. Eventually, I sought refugee in the spiritual blessing of the Messenger of Allah (peace be upon him). Everything became clear. I discovered the secret and was saved."[48]

Likewise, Abraham (peace be upon him) also said: *"I will go to my Lord! He will surely guide me!"* (Qur'an, Saffat, 37/99).

Similarly, Mawlana Jalaluddin Rumi also explained the limit of reason as follows: "Reason takes the ill to the doctor. After that, one needs to submit to the doctor" [49]

In brief, the secrets of the Prophets are beyond reason.

Courtesy, Compassion and Altruism in the Life of the Prophet of Mercy

According to the reports of countless numbers of the companions, Prophet Muhammad (peace be upon him) was

---

(48) Ghazali, Abû Hâmid, *al-Munqiz min al-Dalâl*, (Beirut, 1988), p.60.
(49) Rûmî, Jalâladdin, *Mathnawî Ma'nawî*, (Tehran, 1378), v.IV, 3323.

the best of all humans in morality and courtesy. He was always smiling. There was a shining brightness and light in his face.

Prophet Muhammad (peace be upon him) had such a refined heart that one day when he saw a man spit on the ground, his blessed face became red and he stooped. The companions rushed and covered the spit. Then the Messenger of Allah (peace be upon him) continued on his way.

Prophet Muhammad (peace be upon him) stated that clean dress is an indication of a Muslim's high value in the presence of Allah. He advised white colored dress. He also preferred a white colored shroud. This is because, he explained, it is cleaner, more beautiful and more blessed. The Messenger of Allah who ordered tidy dress and disliked unruly clothes, did not approve of untrimmed hair and beards either. For instance, once a man with untrimmed and uncombed hair and beard came to the Mosque of the Prophet. By pointing with his hand, he gave the man the message to take care of his beard and hair. The man did so by obeying the order of the Prophet (peace be upon him) and he said: "Is not this look nicer than the look of one like the devil with messy hair and beard" [50].

One day, the Prophet (peace be upon him) saw a man with messy hair and beard. In surprise, he asked: "Why does not this man wash and comb his hair?" [51]

Umar ibn Hattab (may Allah be pleased with him) related that:

(50) Muwatta, Shar 7; al-Bayhaqî, Shu'ab al-Îmân, V, 225.
(51) Abû Dâwûd, Libas 13; Nasâî, Zînah 60; Ahmad ibn Hanbal, al-Musnad, III, 357.

"A rude bedouin called Prophet Muhammad (peace be upon him) three times. Each time, he remained courteous to him despite his rudeness and responded to him by saying, 'welcome, please.'"[52]. He was extremely disturbed by messy appearances because of the sensitiveness and depth of his soul.

Another time, he said to a man who came to him with an untidy dress:

"Do you have money? How is your financial condition?" When the man told him that he was well off, he said to the man: "If Allah gave you wealth, let its signs appear on you!" [53]

In another hadith, he said: "Allah is pleased by seeing the signs of wealth he has given to his servant" [54]. These incidents illustrate beautifully how purity of heart and external aesthetic complement each other in Islam.

To protect himself from arrogance and showing off, a Muslim who wears a new dress must be aware that this is a gift from Allah and pray in the manner the Prophet (peace be upon him) did:

"I thank Allah who dressed me in these clothes though I had no power to do so. O Allah! I ask for abundant blessings through this dress and the work I do while dressed in it. I seek refuge in you from the evil of this dress and the evil work which may done with this..." [55]. By praying so, the

---

(52) Tirmidhî, *Zuhd* 50; Ahmad ibn Hanbal, *al-Musnad*, IV, 239; Nasâî, *al-Sunan al-Kubrâ*, VI, 344; al-San'ânî, *al-Musannaf*, I, 206.

(53) Nasâî, *Zînah* 54; Tirmidhî, *Birr* 63; Ahmad ibn Hanbal, *al-Musnad*, IV, 137; Ibn Hibbân, *al-Sahîh*, XII, 234.

(54) Tirmidhî, *Adab* 54; Ahmad ibn Hanbal, *al-Musnad*, II, 311; al-Hâkim, *al-Mustadrak*, IV, 150.

(55) Abû Dâwûd, *Libas* 1; Tirmidhî, *Da'avât* 55; Ibn Mâjah, *At'imah* 16.

Prophet (peace be upon him) expressed his wish to use everything in the path of Allah.

Similarly, Prophet Muhammad (peace be upon him) warned against hellfire by explaining that those who dress up with the purpose of displaying arrogance, showing off and self-love will wear a dress of shame on the last day.

Abdullah ibn Amr, (may Allah be pleased with him), narrated that Prophet Muhammad (peace be upon him) never used the bad expressions commonly used in daily language. The Prophet (peace be upon him) said, "the little matters of courtesy that look easy to you which you take lightly will be very important on the day of judgement".[56]

Once Abu Dharr al-Ghifari called Bilal "the son of a black woman." When the Prophet (peace be upon him) heard that, he said to Abu Dharr al-Ghifari: "O Abu Dharr! You are indeed someone who is still carrying traces of the time of ignorance, Jahliyya"[57].

The Messenger of Allah (peace be upon him) served his guests personally out of courtesy. He did not violate the rules of courtesy even when he was a child. He was known for his compassion and closeness to the needy, the orphans, the widows and the people who had no relatives to assist them[58].

Anas (may Allah be pleased with him) said: "I served

---

(56) Tirmidhî, *Birr* 61; al-Bayhaqî, *al-Sunan al-Kubrâ*, X, 193; Ma'mar ibn Râshid, *al-Jâmi'*, XI, 146; al-Qudâî, *Musnad al-Shihâb*, I, 274.

(57) Bukhârî, *Îmân* 22; Muslim, *Aymân* 38; Abû Dâwûd, *Adab* 124; Tirmidhî, *Tafsir Surah 22*, 1; Ahmad ibn Hanbal, *al-Musnad*, V, 161.

(58) Bukhârî, *Nafaqât* 1; Muslim, *Zuhd* 41-42.

Prophet Muhammad (peace be upon him) for ten years. He never reprimanded me by asking "why did you do so?" when I made mistakes" [59].

His mercy reached even to the captives of war. He ordered their good treatment.

The mercy of the Prophet (peace be upon him) encompassed all creatures. When he saw a child, happiness covered his face and he took the children of his companions in his arms and patted them. He never failed to greet the children, showed them affection and joked with them. Once he saw a group of children who were racing; he joined them and raced with them.

He, who was sent as a mercy to the worlds, took children on his camel when he came across them on the way and paid attention to them. Anas (may Allah be pleased with him) described his conduct as follows: "I have not seen anyone who respected the rights of his family and children more than the Messenger of Allah (peace be upon him)." [60]

Aishah (may Allah be pleased with her) narrated that once, Prophet Muhammad (peace be upon him) was playing with his grandchildren. A bedouin came in. The bedouin was surprised when he saw the scene. He asked: "– O Messenger of Allah! Do you kiss the children? We never kiss our children. Nor do we play with them. Our Guide (peace be upon him) said to him:

(59) Muslim, *Fadâil* 51; Abû Dâwûd, *Adab* 1; Dârimî, *Muqaddimah* 10.
(60) Muslim, *Fadâil* 63; Ahmad ibn Hanbal, *al-Musnad*, III, 112; Ibn Hibbân, *al-Sahîh*, XV, 400; al-Bayhaqî, *al-Sunan al-Kubrâ*, II, 263.

"If Allah took away the compassion and mercy from your heart, what can I do for you?" [61]. This expression illustrates best the position of Islam on the treatment of children.

Prophet Muhammad had Zayd's son Usamah, and his grandson, Hasan, sit on his two knees and while hugging them, he said: "O my Lord! Give mercy and happiness to these! Because I wish happiness and mercy for them" [62]. He also prohibited cursing children. These are some of the signs of his endless mercy for children.

If baby cried while his/her mother was praying, he permitted the mother to shorten her salat in order to prevent the child from crying until she returned [63]. He made prayers entire nights and cried in tears for his community, the Ummah [64]. He sacrificed all his life to save humanity from the hellfire [65]. These are some indications of his deep mercy.

His Exemplary Conduct with People

The Messenger of Allah (peace be upon him) was the perfect example to follow not only with his words but ,more

---

(61) Bukhârî, *Adab* 18; Muslim, *Fadâil* 64; Ibn Mâjah, *Adab* 3; Ahmad ibn Hanbal, *al-Musnad*, VI, 56, 70.

(62) Bukhârî, *Adab*, 18; Muslim, *Fadâil* 64.

(63) Bukhârî, *Azan* 65; Muslim, *Salât* 191; Abû Dâwûd, *Salât* 123; Tirmidhî, *Salât* 159; Nasâî, *Imamah* 35; Ibn Mâjah, *Iqamah* 49; Ahmad ibn Hanbal, *al-Musnad*, III, 109.

(64) Muslim, *Îmân* 346; Ahmad ibn Hanbal, *al-Musnad*, V, 127; Ibn Hibbân, *al-Sahîh*, XVI, 217.

(65) Bukhârî, *Riqâq* 26; Muslim, *Fadâil* 17.

importantly, with his actions. The Messenger of Allah (peace be upon him) was a perfect example for people in all walks of life. He treated everyone with respect. His mercy which encompassed all creatures was endless. He did not spare his tenderness and generous conduct, even from non-Muslims.

Jabir ibn Abdullah narrated that: "One day, people were carrying a corpse. The Messenger of Allah (peace be upon him) stood up. We also did so. Later, we said:

"– O Messenger of Allah! It was the corpse of a Jewish person!"

He responded:

"– Is he not also a human?"[66]

He was a divine mercy, a manifestation of the divine name al-Rahman, who embraced the whole world. His life was an embodiment of the principle "love creatures, for the sake of the Creator."

One day, the companions, as a result of pressures from non-Muslims, asked the Prophet (peace be upon him) to make a prayer for the condemnation of the enemies of Islam by Allah. In response, the Prophet said:

"I did not come for condemnation; I came as a mercy." [67].

The prayer he made against his fiercest enemies was as follows: "O my Lord! They know not! Give them guidance!" [68].

---

(66) Bukhârî, *Janâiz* 50; Muslim, *Janâiz* 81.

(67) Muslim, *Jihâd* 104; Abû Ya'lâ, *al-Musnad*, XI, 35; al-Bayhaqî, *al-Sunan al-Kubrâ*, III, 352; al-Tabarânî, *al-Mu'jam al-Awsat*, III, 223.

(68) Bukhârî, *Anbiyâ* 54; Muslim, *Jihâd* 104; Ibn Mâjah, *Fitan* 33; Ibn Hıbban, *al-Sahîh*, III, 254.

Abdullah Ibn Ubayy was the secret chief of the hypocrites in Medina. He betrayed the Prophet (peace be upon him) on a very critical day by leaving the Muslim army with his followers on the way to the battle of Uhud. Also, he betrayed the Prophet (peace be upon him) and the community of believers on many other occasions.

As a result of hidden divine wisdom, Abdullah's son, unlike his father, was a most sincere believer. When Abdullah ibn Ubayy died, his son came to the Prophet and asked for his shirt to wrap his father's corpse in with the hope that he might receive some blessing from it. Rasullullah (peace be upon him) did not break the heart of his companion and gave him his shirt to be used in covering the corpse of a hypocrite [69] who had also been a protagonist in the incident of Ifk where the blessed wife of the Prophet, Aishah was slandered.

Is it possible to find a parallel example of humanity and kindness in world history?

Muhammad (peace be upon him) was the most excellent example of mercy. Once in salat, he heard a bedouin praying, "O my Lord! Bless Muhammad and me alone, but not others!" After the salat, the Prophet said to him: "You are narrowing what is large." [70]

Rasulullah (peace be upon him) was not a human being who belonged exclusively to his time and the people living around

---

(69) Bukhârî, *Janâiz* 23; Muslim, *Munafiqun* 4; Abû Dâwûd, *Janâiz* 1; Nasâî, *Janâiz* 40; Ahmad ibn Hanbal, *al-Musnad* II, 18.

(70) Bukhârî, *Adab* 27; Ibn Mâjah, *Taharah* 78; Ahmad ibn Hanbal, *al-Musnad*, II, 239.

him. He stood at a point where he could unite all humanity under the banner of love, mercy and happiness by merging them in the light of Islam and by transforming the environment of hardened hearts, of bigotry and of racism. The success he showed in this regard is the brightest page of human history.

From this perspective, he became the best educator for all of humanity as a consequence of the blessed divine education he had received. The oppressors who buried their daughters alive and treated their slaves in a merciless way found guidance under the dome of his mercy. This education was so effective that some of these people gained enough integrity and virtue to become the most distinguished people in the world.

Our Prophet Muhammad (peace be upon him) assisted all people without discrimination and according to their needs. The following incident reflects this.

One day a bedouin came to him for help. He gave him everything he had with him, and asked: "Does this satisfy you?"

The bedouin, who had little courtesy, said: "No! You did not give me enough!"

Then, some of the companions got angry with him because of his rudeness and wanted to reprimand him. Rasulullah (peace be upon him), however, stopped them from doing so. He took the bedouin with him and went to his home. He gave some more charity to the bedouin and asked:

"Could this please you?"

The bedouin was happy this time. He said: "Yes! May Allah give you abundant blessings on behalf of me, my family and my relatives!"

After pleasing the bedouin, the Prophet (peace be upon him) with the purpose of removing the negative feeling between the bedouin and his companions, said to him:

"You said what you said in the beginning because you thought what we gave was too little for you. For this reason, my companions may have developed some negative feelings towards you. When we return to them, repeat what you just said so that the negative feelings in their hearts will vanish."

When they came back to the place where the companions were, the bedouin turned to the Prophet (peace be upon him) and said to him: "May Allah give you abundant blessings on behalf of me, my family and my relatives!"

After the bedouin left, the Prophet (peace be upon him) turned to his companions and said to them: "The incident which has taken place between me and this bedouin resembles that of the person who had a camel which escaped from him. When a crowd of people ran after the camel to catch it, it got more scared. Then the owner of the camel called the crowd: "Please leave me and my camel alone! I know it better than you and I treat it better than you do." He walked alone towards his camel. He collected some dates from the ground and gave them to the camel. The camel came to him and followed him. He put the pack-saddle on the camel, mounted it and left riding it. Similarly, if I had listened to you when the bedouin said what he said, the miserable bedouin was going to go to the hellfire." [71].

This statement is important with respect to the messages it contains regarding human education. It is necessary to take the psychology of human beings into consideration. Then the paths leading to the heart of the person can be discovered. One should try to reach his goal by proceeding along these paths. Otherwise, one's attempt to educate will be counterproductive and increase the already existing adversity.

Another lesson we may learn from this incident is as follows: humans are overcome by kindness and generosity because they are created weak. The one who is treated generously becomes lesser of an enemy if he is already an enemy; if he is in the middle, he becomes a friend; if he is already a friend, he becomes a closer friend.

Our ancestors said: "The hospitality even of a cup of coffee is remembered with gratitude for forty years."

The Courtesy of the Prophet of Mercy towards the Needy

The Prophet (peace be upon him) behaved with compassion towards the needy in order to compensate for their shortage of material wealth. Abdullah ibn Amr narrated the following story:

"One day, the Prophet (peace be upon him) came to the masjid. The poor were sitting to a side. He went and sat among them to honor them. He chatted with them and said: 'Good

---

(71) al-Marwazî (d.294), *Ta'zîm qadr al-salât*, II, 931; al-Haythamî, *Majma' al-zawâid*, IX, 160.

tiding be to the poor Immigrants! They will enter the gardens of Paradise forty years earlier than the rich. The reckoning of the poor on the day of Judgement will end sooner than the rich because they do not have money and property'" [72].

Rasulullah (peace be upon him) made the following prayer frequently because of his concern about the heavy responsibility of reckoning in the Hereafter.

"O my Lord! Make me live as the poor. Let me die as the poor. Resurrect me among the poor" [73].

All Prophets will go the Paradise. Yet, each one will be questioned about the bountiful blessings given to them and the message they were entrusted to convey to their communities. The following verse from the Qur'an explains that everyone including the Prophets, will be questioned: *"Then shall we question those to whom Our Message was sent and those to whom we sent it"* (Qur'an, Araf, 7/6).

For instance, the Prophet Suleiman (peace be upon him) will enter Paradise after all other Prophets because he was given wealth and kingship which will cause his questioning to continue longer.

There were the rich among the companions of the Prophet (peace be upon him) as well. They gained the praise of the Prophet by not sparing their wealth or lives in the path of Allah. Furthermore, Allah also gave them good tidings in

---

(72) Tirmidhî, *Zuhd* 37; Dârimî, *Riqâq* 118; Ahmad ibn Hanbal, *al-Musnad*, III, 63; Nasâî, *al-Sunan al-Kubrâ*, III, 443; al-Bayhaqî, *al-Sunan al-Kubrâ*, VII, 12.

(73) Tirmidhî, *Zuhd* 37; Ibn Mâjah, *Zuhd* 7; al-Hâkim, *al-Mustadrak*, IV, 358; al-Bayhaqî, *al-Sunan al-Kubrâ*, VII, 12.

the following verse: *"Allah has purchased of the Believers their person and their goods; for theirs (in return) is the Garden (of Paradise): They fight in His cause, and slay and are slain: A promise binding on Him in Truth, through the Torah, the Gospel, and the Qur'an: And who is more faithful to his covenant than Allah? Then rejoice the bargain which ye have concluded; that is the achievement supreme"* (Qur'an, Tawba, 9/111).

⁂

One of the wealthy was the closest friend of the Prophet, Abu Bakr, who, despite his wealth, led a most humble life. He was described by Allah in the Qur'an as the "second of the two." He occupied a respected place among the tradesmen of the Quraysh. According to Aishah (may Allah be pleased with her), he also did not leave a dirham (silver money) nor a dinar (gold money) when he passed away. He bequeathed only a camel and a slave who knew how to make swords. In his will to his daughter, he stressed that this slave be given to Umar, the next Caliph after him. He used his wealth in the most beneficial way by putting it in the service of the Messenger of Allah, spending his money in the Cause of Truth. Particularly, in the first years of Islam, which was the most challenging time, he purchased and freed Muslim slaves who were being tortured by their disbelieving owners for accepting Islam.

His wealth did not prevent him from having abstention, zuhd, from worldly pleasures. On the contrary, by using his wealth appropriately, he became one of the prime examples of how to lead a life of abstention in spite of one's wealth. For this reason, the Messenger of Allah showed regard for his wealth and said about him:

"We paid back all the favors we received from the people except those from Abu Bakir. The place of his favor to us is so huge that Allah will reward him for that on the Day of Judgement. I did not benefit from the wealth of anyone more than the wealth of Abu Bakr. If I were to choose an intimate friend, I would choose Abu Bakr" [74].

❦

The Prophet Muhammad (peace be upon him) said:

"Humans are equal like the tooth of a comb except for piety where the difference between humans lies" [75].

The blessed companions once had been divided along tribal lines, for racial reasons, as master and slave, and as rich and poor. They had been fragmented into classes and had been ready to shed each other's blood. Yet, after they were honored by accepting Islam, they lived in a climate of legendary brotherhood under the abundant blessing of the sublime principle stated in this hadith.

To put it more concretely, recall the following incident. After the conquering of Mecca, the Messenger of Allah (peace be upon him) decided to attack Byzantium for a second time. He assigned Zayd's son, Usamah, as the commander of the army. Usamah was only twenty one years old and the son of a freed slave. The departure of the army was delayed because of the demise of the Prophet (peace be

---

(74) Tirmidhî, *Manâqib* 15; Ibn Mâjah, *Muqaddimah* 11; Ahmad ibn Hanbal, *al-Musnad*, II, 253, 366; Ibn Hibbân, *al-Sahîh*, XV, 273.

(75) âl-Qudâî, *Musnad al-Shihâb*, I, 145; al-Hatîb al-Bagdâdî, *Târîkhu Bagdâd*, VII, 57; Ibn 'Adiyy, *al-Kâmil fî al-du'afâ*, III, 248; Ibn Hibbân, *al-Majrûhîn*, I, 198; Ibn Hagar al-'Asqalânî, *Lisân al-mîzân*, II, 42.

THE PROPHET OF MERCY

upon him). Yet the new Caliph, Abu Bakr, ordered the army to proceed as planned by the Prophet before his departure from this world. Some of the great companions of the Prophet and some of the nobility of the Quraysh walked behind this young commander who was only twenty years old. Even Abu Bakr, inspite of being the Caliph, accompanied him until the end of Medina, and strikingly, on foot... Usamah got off from his horse and invited Abu Bakr to ride his horse, yet, he responded as follows: "O Usamah! The Messenger of Allah assigned you. Let my feet gain some dust in the path of Allah!" [76].

As we see, those who were gifted by the divine honor of being raised at the blessed hands of the Prophet (peace be upon him) were never discriminated with such titles as slave, poor, rich, master, young, old, etc. These terms were rejected and instead any believer was free to ascend to a high level dependent only on his sincerity and spiritual merit.

Ma'rur son of Suwayd told the following story:

"I saw Abu Dharr with a cloth on him. His slave was also dressed the same way. I asked him the reason. He related that the Prophet (peace be upon him) said:

"Slaves are your brothers entrusted by Allah to your service. If one of you has his brother under his service, let him feed his brother from his own food, and dress him from his own kind. Do not give them responsibility for things beyond their power. If you do so, help them." [77].

---

(76) Ibn Kathîr, *al-Bidâyah van-nihâyah*, III, 309.
(77) Bukhârî, *Îmân* 22; Muslim, *Aymân* 40; Abû Dâwûd, *Adab* 124; Tirmidhî, *Birr* 29; Ahmad ibn Hanbal, *al-Musnad*, V, 58, 161

❦

One day, the Messenger of Allah, remembered a black slave and asked about him:

"What did that person do? I have not seen him for a while."

"He died, O Messenger of Allah," they responded. The Prophet (peace be upon him) reprimanded them: "Why didn't you let me know?"

The companions then told him what had happened to that slave. They had not considered the incident very important and thought it was a usual event. The Messenger of Allah (peace be upon him) said: "Show me his grave!"

Then he went to his grave and prayed the funeral prayer. [78]

The Messenger of Allah (peace be upon him) took a special pleasure from freeing slaves and elevating them to the level of other people. The best example of this was his relationship with Zayd ibn Haritha, who was a gift to him by our blessed mother, Khadija. He freed Zayd and gave him the right to choose between him and his parents. Zayd chose the Prophet (peace be upon him) though he was passing through a difficult time facing torture and negative propaganda of the Quraysh against him. Later, this companion reached so high a level among the companions that the Prophet (peace be upon him) assigned him as the commander of the army in the war of Tabuk against the

---

(78) Bukhârî, *Salât* 72; Muslim, *Janâiz* 71; Abû Dâwûd, *Janâiz* 57 ; Ibn Mâjah, *Janâiz* 32; Ahmad ibn Hanbal, *al-Musnad,* II, 353, 388.

Byzantine. He reached the level of martyr in this war and bequeathed to the following generations a brilliant life like a star. [79] Briefly put, his life was like the life of Prophet Joseph (peace be upon him) who was elevated from slavery to kingship.

The Messenger of Allah never accepted the abuse of slaves. He said that:

"Those who abuse their slaves cannot enter Paradise"[80].

The mercy of the Prophet toward the slaves reached such a level that he refused to call them as "slave" or "maid", instead he advised and commanded Muslims to call them as "my son" or "my daughter" [81].

He himself used to go among the slaves, talk to them, visit their ill, accept their invitations, and attend their funeral services.

Abu Davud relates that the following were the last words of the Prophet (peace be upon him): "Pay great attention to salat! Fear Allah for the slaves you own!" (Abu Davud, Adab, 124).

❀

All of the companions aimed to completely internalize the perfect manners of the Prophet. The following incident reflects the feelings of loyalty and generosity Umar (may

(79) Ibn Hagar al-'Asqalânî, al-İsâbah fi tamyîz al-sahâbah, II, 598-601; Ibn Abdilbarr, al-İstî'âb fî ma'rifatil-ashâb, II, 542-546.

(80) Tirmidhî, Birr 29; Ibn Mâjah, Adab 10; Ahmad b. Hanbal, al-Musnad, I, 7; al-Tabarânî, al-Mu'jam al-Awsat, IX, 124; Abû Ya'lâ, al-Musnad, I, 94.

(81) Bukhârî, Itk 17; Muslim, Alfaz 13, 15; ; Abû Dâwûd, Adab 75; Ahmad b. Hanbal, al-Musnad, II, 316, 423.

Allah be pleased with him) had. Aslam, one of the companions, related that:

"One day, I went to the market place with Umar ibn al-Khattab (may Allah be pleased with him). A young woman approached Umar (may Allah be pleased with him) from behind and said to him:

"– Oh, Amir of the Believers! My husband died and left some children. By God, they cannot do anything. They cannot even take care of themselves. They have no land to cultivate, nor an animal to milk. I am afraid that poverty and hunger will finish their life like a wild animal. I am the daughter of Huffaf ibn Ayma al-Ghifari. My father was present at the Hudaybiya Agreement…"

When Umar (may Allah be pleased with him) heard these words, he said:

"Such a great honor!"

Then he went to the place where the animals donated as zakat were kept. He loaded two huge sacks of food on a sturdy camel. Between these two sacks, he put more food and some clothes. He put the halter of the camel in the woman's hand and said to her:

"Take the camel. Before you finish all this, Allah will open a door of blessing for you." He prayed for her.

One of the people near to him said:

"Oh, Amir of Believers! You gave too much to that woman!"

Umar responded by saying:

"His father was present at the Hudaybiya with the

Prophet (peace be upon him). By God, I witnessed myself that the father and brother of this woman laid siege to a castle and conquered it. When they conquered the castle, we also got our share from the bounty." [82].

The following incident is a a ray of light reflecting the nature of the heart of Umar (may Allah be pleased with him).

From the companions, Aslam narrated that "One night we were walking for inspection on the hill of Waqim in Medina. We saw a woman with children in a home. The children were crying. There was a bowl filled with water in the fire place. Umar (may Allah be pleased with him) asked the woman why the children were crying. She said: "out of hunger".

Umar's eyes became full of tears when he learned that instead of soup there was nothing boiling in the water except stones. This was a trick the woman had devised to cheat the children so they would sleep. He immediately went to the storage house where the charity was stored. He personally filled a big sack with flour and carried it on his own shoulders to the family. I wanted to shoulder the sack, but he refused by saying,

"Oh, Aslam! I will carry it. I will be asked about these children in the Hereafter."

When we went to the home of the woman, he also undertook the cooking. He was on the one hand blowing the fire and on the other stirring the soup. I even saw that the smoke reached to his beard. This way, he cooked the food.

---

(82) Bukhârî, *Magâzî* 35.

Then he served the food to children. When the children became full he sat across them. He was awesome, like a lion. I was afraid to say anything. He stayed until the children started laughing and playing.

Then he stood up and said:

"Oh, Aslam! Do you know why I sat across from them? When I saw them they were crying. I did not want to leave them before seeing them laugh. When I saw them laugh, I felt comfortable."

It should be known that grateful, humble, generous rich people acting in accordance with the needs of humanity are honored equally by Allah with patient poor people who act with dignity. Generosity and mercy lead people to happiness in the Hereafter by protecting them from the difficulties of this world. Likewise, good tidings are awaiting those who spiritually carry the pain of patience.

The following hadith illustrates very well how to practice gratefulness and patience which have to be applied in various arenas of life in order to reach perfection of heart.

"I admire a believer whose entire activity consists of good behavior. Such a quality does not exist except with the Believer. He shows gratefulness when he receives a blessing from Allah, which is good for him. Likewise, if a difficulty reaches him, he shows patience, which is also good for him" [83].

One day, when the Prophet (peace be upon him) was sitting in Medina, members of a miserable tribe came. They had no shoes. Their skin was stuck to their bones because of

---

(83) Muslim, *Zuhd* 64; Ahmad ibn Hanbal, *al-Musnad*, VI, 16; Ibn Hibbân, *al-Sahîh*, VII, 155.

hunger. The Prophet (peace be upon him) became very sad upon seeing their condition and his color changed. He had Bilal (may Allah be pleased with him) give the adhan and gathered his companions. From his companions, he took up a collection for the tribe, generously helping them [84].

In a society one will intrinsically find poor, rich and middle class people. Both, in the verses of the Qur'an and the teachings of the Prophet (peace be upon him), one may find Islamic principles concerning the relationship of these groups. The patient poor and the grateful rich are two groups praised by Allah and the Prophet (pbuh).

The purpose of the rich is to give in charity of what Allah has given to them and, for the poor, to show patience in the best way for what Allah has deprived them of. Abdurrahman ibn Awf, Abu Bakr and people like them serve as the best examples of the grateful rich. Likewise, Abu Dharr al-Ghifari, Abu al-Darda and people like them are the examples of the patient poor. The life styles of both groups were more or less the same because their views of life were defined by the principle that all "property belongs to Allah."

For this reason, Islam does not criticize the righteous poor nor the rich, but it gives good tidings of gaining paradise by remaining thankful to Allah.

As a consequence of the lives of the disadvantaged, Allah provides sustenance and blessings to His community. For the sake of the poor, Allah helps the community in abundance. The Messenger of Allah (peace be upon him) said regarding this issue:

---

(84) Muslim, *Zakât* 69, 70; Ahmad ibn Hanbal, *al-Musnad*, IV, 358, 361.

"Allah helps this community for the sake of the prayers of the weak, their salat and their sincerity" [85].

Based on this truth, the Messenger of Allah began wars with the prayers of poor Muslims because he expected triumph as a result of their sincerity. When he saw the needy situation of the People of Suffa, he said:

"If you had known what is prepared in the presence of Allah for you, you would wish for the increase of your deprivation" [86]. He praised them and demonstrated the importance he assigned to poverty.

Similarly, taking into consideration the financial hardship Muslims were in, he said; "A human has no right to more than a house to give him shelter, bread to feed himself, a cloth to cover his private parts and some water to drink" [87].

He also stated that the first to drink from the river of Kawthar in the Hereafter will be the poor [88] and Allah loves those who exercise patience and reliance on Allah despite their poverty.

Furthermore, Prophet Muhammad stated, "There are many people among you with messy hair and beards and poor appearance. Yet, if they pray, Allah accepts their prayers and would not turn them down. Bara ibn Malik is one of them" [89].

(85) Bukhârî, *Jihâd* 76; Abû Dâwûd, *Jihâd* 70; Tirmidhî, *Jihâd* 24; Nasâî, *Jihâd* 43; Ahmad ibn Hanbal, *al-Musnad*, I, 173.

(86) Tirmidhî, *Zuhd* 39; Ibn Hibbân, *al-Sahîh*, II, 502; al-Bazzâr, *al-Musnad*, IX, 205; al-Tabarânî, *al-Mu'jam al-Kabîr*, XVIII, 310.

(87) Tirmidhî, *Zuhd* 30; Ahmad ibn Hanbal, *al-Musnad*, I, 62; al-Kissî, *Musnad 'Abd ibn Humayd*, I, 46; al-Hâkim, *al-Mustadrak*, IV, 347; al-Bayhaqî, *Shu'ab al-Îmân*, V, 157.

(88) Tirmidhî, *Qiyâmah* 15.

(89) Tirmidhî, *Manâqib* 54; Ma'mar ibn Râshid, *al-Jâmi'*, XI, 306; al-Bazzâr, *al-Musnad*, V, 404; al-Tabarânî, *al-Mu'jam al-Awsat*, I, 264.

Bara, who was the brother of Anas, had no place to stay, nor any food to eat. His food was barely sufficient to keep him alive. Those people who accept poverty with happiness are among the ones whose prayers Allah accepts. The companions who knew what the Prophet (peace be upon him) had said about Bara, asked him to make a special prayer for them as they were about to lose a war during the reign of Umar. He made a prayer and said:

"By God! Tomorrow you will be given triumph and I will be martyred!..."

Indeed, the next day Muslims triumphed and Bara received the mercy of the Most Merciful Allah, al-Rahman, by becoming a martyr, which he had longed for, for a long time. Thus with this occurrence we may see yet one more miracle of the Prophet (peace be upon him). [90]

❀

The life of Prophet Muhammad (peace be upon him) is full of miracles, honesty, trustworthiness, loyalty, tenderness, compassion and courtesy. He said to his wife Aishah:

"O Aishah! Show compassion to the poor! Keep them near to you so that Allah also keeps you near to him on the Day of Judgement!..."

He advised her as follows:

"O Aishah! Never turn away a beggar empty handed from your door; protect yourself from the Hellfire even with half a date!" [91].

(90) Ibn Abdilbarr, *al-Istî'âb*, I, 154; Ibn Hagar al-'Asqalânî, *al-Isâbah*, I, 281.
(91) Tirmidhî, *Zuhd* 37; al-Bayhaqî, *al-Sunan al-Kubrâ*, VII, 12.

Gradual Education of the People by the Prophet

Islam is an evolving system. Consequently, it does not require rejection of previous good institutional examples; instead it develops their positive aspects and reforms their negative aspects. It sees no harm in preserving positive aspects of the past based on clearly set criteria. Using these criteria, it tries to revive an institution rather than throwing it away.

Only those who are confident with themselves and their cause gradually implement changes which are usually rapidly integrated and transform the social order. This type of gradual approach does not overburden societies right away. As a result, possible negative reactions are forestalled. The best example of this approach is the way Islam reformed slavery. Islam transformed the institution of slavery and made it only a nominal identity. Islam had framed the institution of slavery within virtuous principles in such a way that would eventually lead to its annihilation.

Islam preserved slavery only as a name and only for a temporary period of time with an aim to ending it. Thus, to accuse Islam of defending slavery is a result of ignorance and bigotry. In classical Islamic law, for the atonement of some sins, freeing a slave was required. Having set this principle, Islam elevated the slaves from being mere tools in the hands of their owners. There was left little difference between a free man and a slave. The Prophet (peace be upon him) was the first to apply the principle of sharing the same food and the same cloth with one's slave. The institution of slavery, which used to be an institution of oppression, lost this quality as Islam emphasized respect for the rights of all people.

The Prophet (peace be upon him) ordered the owner of the slaves to educate them and to help them get married after freeing them. He warned that those who mistreated their slaves would not be able to enter Paradise.

He encouraged the freeing of slaves and said that this was a great worship of Allah. One day, he witnessed that Abu Dharr treated his slave harshly without knowing. He became very sad and asked Abu Dharr:

"O Abu Dharr! Do you still carry the traces of the time of ignorance before the coming of true religion?" He continued by saying: "Don't treat the creatures of Allah harshly! If they do not fit your temperament, free them. Do not overburden them! If you overburden, then, help them" (92).

A man married his slave with his slave girl. Yet, later he wanted them to divorce. The slave complained to the Prophet, who said to the owner of the slave:

"The rights of marriage and divorce are not yours; do not interfere!"(93)

The Messenger of Allah repeatedly asked his companions to forgive the mistakes of their slaves. Once a slave girl lost the money her owner gave her to buy flour. She could not return home because she was afraid of getting punished. She was crying on the sidewalk. When the Prophet (peace be upon him) had listened to her story, he gave her the same amount of money she had lost and took her back home

(92) Bukhârî, Îmân 22; Muslim, Aymân 38; Abû Dâwûd, Adab 124; Tirmidhî, Birr 29; Ibn Mâjah, Adab 10; Ahmad ibn Hanbal, al-Musnad, IV, 36.
(93) Ibn Mâjah, Talak 31; al-Bayhaqî, al-Sunan al-Kubrâ, VII, 360, 370; al-Daraqutni, al-Sunan, IV, 37; al-Tabarânî, al-Mu'jam al-Kabîr, XI, 300.

because he was not sure about the treatment she would receive from her owners. He gave them advice about being compassionate. The companions, as a result of the advice they received, forgave the slave girl.

Another point that needs to be noted is that the reason Islam accepted the legitimacy of slavery was because of the existence of wars that were impossible to quail. One of the expected outcomes of wars were captives and slaves. Since Islam is distinguished by mercy and compassion, it encourages equal treatment of slaves and free people. Zayd, inspite of the fact that he was set free by the Prophet (peace be upon him), preferred to stay with the Prophet until his death and Zayd refused to return home to his parents.

Prophet Muhammad (peace be upon him) said;

"Give the person who is cooking for you his share! Let him sit next to you! Eat with him! If you cannot do that, take a piece of bread, dunk it in the plate and put it in his mouth and offer him food. Allah, the Most High, assigned them as servants and slaves for you. If he wished he could have made you their servants!" [94]

Since they were so afraid of violating human rights, most of the companions freed their slaves. These examples exemplify how Islam provided humanity with a matchless standard of virtue.

The Conduct of the Prophet of Mercy with Women

In the pre-Islamic era, women had been treated in a way such that their womanly pride was offended. Concubines

---

(94) For similiar hadith See, Bukhârî, Îmân 22; Muslim, Aymân 38; Abû Dâwûd, Adab 124; al-Bayhaqî, al-Sunan al-Kubrâ, VIII, 36.

were seen as an instrument of amusement in a very degrading way. Fearing that they would become prostitutes, little girls were buried alive without any mercy. With petrified hearts, even worse crimes were committed in order to protect them from a calamity which is the result of ignorance. Allah describes their behavior as follows:

"When news is brought to one of them, of (the birth of) a female (child), his face darkens, and he is filled with inward grief. With shame does he hide himself from his people, because of the bad news he has had received! Shall he retain it on (sufferance and) contempt or bury it in the dust? Ah! What an evil (choice) they decide on?" (Qur'an, Nahl, 16/58-59).

By the order of Prophet Muhammad, women's rights were established. Women became the example of modesty and virtue in society. The institution of motherhood gained honor. With the hadith which says "Paradise lies under the feet of the mothers"[95], mothers earned the status they deserved by the courtesy of Prophet Muhammad.

The following example of the kindness extended by the Prophet to women is a beautiful one. "During a journey, a slave named Anjasha raced the camels by singing [96]. Prophet Muhammad, thinking of the possibility that the delicate bodies of the ladies on the camels might get hurt, said: O Anjasha! Mind the crystals! Mind the crystals!" [97].

Furthermore, Prophet Muhammad (peace be upon him)

(95) Nasâî, *Jihâd* 6; Ahmad ibn Hanbal, *al-Musnad*, III, 429; *Ibn Mâjah, Jihâd* 12; al-Qudâî, *Musnad al-Shihâb*, I, 102; al-Daylami, *al-Firdaws*, II, 116.
(96) Camels like beautiful voices and singing. The herdsmen for the camels sing to race the camels.
(97) Bukhârî, *Adab* 95; Ahmad ibn Hanbal, *al-Musnad*, III, 117.

in another hadith said; "In this world, women and nice fragrances are made pleasant for me while salat is made the light of my eyes" [98]. Women and nice fragrances are important blessings of Allah in this world.

The importance of a righteous woman in a happy and peaceful religious household is clear. Although today's world has changed, traditionally she protected the family's wealth, organized the house, protected the progeny and protected the family's honor. It was principally the mother of the house who filled the family with happiness. The atmosphere of happiness was dependent on her smile. All worries of the children ended with a compassionate look from the mother. Is there a place more compassionate than the heart of the mother?

Mothers are the creatures who have been granted the highest amount of divine mercy from the Creator. The sovereignty of women begins when they become virtuous mothers. The hadith which states "Paradise lies under the feet of the mothers" is the highest compliment of the Prophet (peace be upon him) to mothers.

Nice fragrance revives the soul with its delicacy. This is a pleasure even the angels enjoy. Salat is the divine union between the servant and the Lord. It is the ascension (miraj) for the soul.

In another hadith, Rasulullah (peace be upon him) said; "The best among you is the one who treats his family the best"[99]. Rasulullah (peace be upon him) also said; "Whatever

---

(98) Nasâî, 'Ishratu'n-nisa 10; Ahmad ibn Hanbal, al-Musnad, III, 128, 199.
(99) Tirmidh, Rada 11; Ibn Mâjah, Nikah 50; Dârimî, Nikah 55; Ahmad ibn Hanbal, al-Musnad, II, 472.

a person spends for himself, his wife and his children is rewarded by Allah as his charity." [100] The Prophet (peace be upon him) has stated in the above teachings that a healthy family can only be based on a foundation of love.

The Conduct of the Prophet of Mercy with Animals

The people of the pre-Islamic era treated animals without any pity or mercy. While still alive they used to cut off pieces of their flesh or their tails. They used to organize brutal animal fights. The Prophet (peace be upon him) put an end to these cruel scenes. The traditions today of cockfights, camel fights and of bull fights originated in the pre-Islamic era.

One day, Rasulullah (peace be upon him) saw a donkey on the road whose face was branded (cauterized). He became very sorry and said; "May God's punishment be upon the person who branded it!" [101]. He recommended that branding for the purpose of marking should be done in a place on an animal's body where it would not hurt the animal to an extreme.

Once he saw a camel which was just skin and bones. He said to the owner of that camel; "Be afraid of Allah about these animals which cannot talk! Do not let them stay hungry!" [102].

Abdullah ibn Ja'far (may Allah be pleased with him)

---

(100) Ibn Mâjah, *Ticârât* 1; Ahmad ibn Hanbal, *al-Musnad*, V, 279; al-Bayhaqî, *al-Sunan al-Kubrâ*, X, 242; Al-Tabarânî, *al-Mu'jam al-Kabîr*, VIII, 239.

(101) Bukhârî, *Zabâih* 25.

(102) Abû Dâwûd, *Jihâd* 47; Ibn Khuzaymah, *al-Sahîh*, IV, 143.

stated, "One day, Rasulullah (peace be upon him) came to the garden of a companion. The camel in that garden moaned and tears began to fall from its eyes when it saw the Prophet. The Messenger of Allah approached the camel and patted its head. The camel stopped moaning. Then the Prophet met the owner of the garden and asked him, are you not afraid of Allah who entrusted you with this camel? It complained to me that you beat and torture it."

❦

Rasulullah (peace be upon him) explained the difference between the states of the merciful and the states of merciless as follows:

"A sinful woman saw a dog in the desert which was licking the sand with its tongue out of thirst. She had pity on it and pulled some water from a well with her shoe and gave it to the dog. Allah forgave her sins because of that. Another woman did not care about her cat and left it hungry for a long time. She did not even let the cat eat the bugs on the soil. Finally, the cat died of hunger. This woman became one of the people of the Hellfire because of her cruelty!" (103)

The Prophet (peace be upon him) transformed an ignorant society into a community that became part of the Age of Happiness (asr al-sa'adah). The people who treated badly their fellow human beings and who buried their daughters alive, were becoming merciful and this extended to the animals as well. This is because the Prophet (peace be upon him) respected even the rights of little sparrows.

---

(103) Bukhârî, *Anbiyâ* 54; Muslim, *Salâm* 151, 154; *Birr* 133; Nasâî, *Kusûf* 14.

Abdurrahman, the son of Abdullah, reports,

"While we were on a journey with Rasulullah (peace be upon him), we saw a sand grouse with its two little babies. We took the babies and the bird began to fly on top of our heads. The Prophet immediately came and said: "Who hurt this bird by taking its babies? Return them to their nest!" [104].

Hunting is permissible in Islamic law. Nonetheless, the Prophet (peace be upon him) warned hunters that they should be careful about the breeding and the reproduction times of animals for the purpose of maintaining ecological balance. Hunting randomly, saddening the young by the death of their mothers or saddening the mothers by the loss of their young disturbs a compassionate and merciful heart.

These hadiths bring to light the fact that the mercy of a perfect believer must be expansive enough to encompass even the wild animals. Therefore, it is commanded in Islam that even the harmful animals like snakes and scorpions should be killed in one shot, with the express purpose of saving them from prolonged suffering. Is not the advice to be merciful even in the killing of harmful animals an example of matchless mercy?

Besides ordering the Believers to be merciful towards animals, the Prophet (peace be upon him) did not like them to be cursed. For example, on the way to Batnubuwat for a military engagement, a man from the Ansar (Helpers) cursed a camel for going to slowly while riding a camel he shared

---

(104) Abû Dâwûd, *Jihâd*, 122; Ahmad ibn Hanbal, *al-Musnad*, I, 404; Hakim, *al-Mustadrak*, IV, 267; al-Tabarânî, *al-Mu'jam al-Awsat*, IV, 261.

with a friend. Rasulullah (peace be upon him) told the Ansari to get off the camel and said to him, "Do not accompany us with the cursed camel any longer! Do not curse yourselves, your children or your property!" [105].

This hadith exemplifies his boundlessness of mercy in Islam [106]. Bayazid-i Bistami, who was known as the "Sultan of the Saints" became so sensitive and refined through practicing the principle of love for creatures for the sake of the Creator, that he felt their pain in his heart. The following story illustrates how deep his feelings were.

During a trip, he rested under a tree and after sometime he stood up and went on his way. After having departed, he noticed that some ants from the place where he had rested were still on his bag. He returned to the same place and dropped the ants at the same point because he hated to take them away from their homes.

This is exemplifies an internalization of the example of the Prophet (peace be upon him). The teachings of the Prophet (peace be upon him) are full of statements that include warnings and provide guidance on this issue. He

---

(105) Muslim, *Zuhd* 74; Ibn Hibbân, *al-Sahîh*, XIII, 52.

(106) Claude Farer wrote about the implications of Islamic morality which commands mercy and compassion to all creatures: "You can understand whether the neighborhood you are passing through is Muslim or Christian by looking at the attitude of the local dogs and cats. If the dogs and cats want to play with you and show closeness to you, you can say with confidence that it is a Muslim neighborhood; if they take a defensive position against you, it must be a non-Muslim neighborhood." This picture, which was provided by a Christian tourist, is an obvious reflection of "love, mercy and compassion to creatures for the sake of the Creator."

said: "One who is deprived of mercy is deprived of all sorts of goodness..." [(107)].

The most distinctive quality of a Muslim is mercy. In the "basmalah", (Bismillahi'r-Rahmani'r-Rahim, which means; in the name of Allah, the most Merciful, the most Compassionate) which we repeat before any deed, Allah reminds us that He is the Most Merciful. Mercy is a deep personality trait of a true Muslim.

In the following incident, Fudayl ibn Iyad, who was one of the Friends of Allah, set an example of how a Muslim should feel in his heart.

They saw him crying and asked:

"Why do you cry?" He responded:

"– I cry because I feel sorry on behalf of a Muslim who wronged me! My sorrow comes from my concern that he will go to the Hellfire because of me."

These incidents are extremely refined manifestations of the inner manners of a heart following the example of Prophet Muhammad (peace be upon him). Prophet Muhammad (peace be upon him) said, "Show mercy to those on the earth so that those in the heavens will show mercy to you!"[(108)]

The Conduct of the Prophet of Mercy with Orphans

In one Hadith it is stated, "The best home is a home in which an orphan is well treated and the worst home is a

---

(107) Muslim, *Birr* 75; Abû Dâwûd, *Adab* 11; Ibn Mâjah, *Adab* 9; Ahmad ibn Hanbal, *al-Musnad*, IV, 362; Ibn Hibbân, *al-Sahîh*, II, 308.

(108) Tirmidhî, *Birr* 16; al-Hâkim, *al-Mustadrak*, IV, 277; al-Bayhaqî, *al-Sunan al-Kubrâ*, IX, 41.

home in which an orphan is maltreated" [109]. In the Qur'an there are many verses concerning nice treatment of the orphans. Allah, the Most High, commands us to be very sensitive towards the orphans.

"Treat not the orphan with harshness!" (Qur'an, Duha, 93/9).

"Whoever pats an orphan's head will be rewarded for every hair his hand touches" [110]. The Prophet repeatedly emphasized the importance of our fulfillment of these important social responsibilities.

It is stated in another hadith that, "I and those who treat well their daughters and sons under their care, will be together in the Paradise" [111]. While saying this, he put together his two fingers.

A complaint reached the Prophet (peace be upon him) about the harshness of someone. As a cure, he recommended the following deed to that person:

"Let him pat the head of the orphans and feed the poor!" [112]

Since Prophet Muhammad (peace be upon him) was raised as an orphan, having been an orphan gained him status and honor in this world and the next. The poet, Mehmed Aslan, describes nicely the feeling of an orphan:

---

(109) Ibn Mâjah, *Adab* 6; al-Kissî, *Musnad Abd ibn Humayd*, I, 427; Bukhârî, *al-Ababul-murfad*, I, 61.

(110) Ahmad ibn Hanbal, *al-Musnad*, V, 250, 265; al-Tabarânî, *al-Mu'jam al-Awsat*, III, 285, *al-Mu'jam al-Kabîr*, VIII, 202; Ibn Abî 'Âsım, *Kitab al-zuhd*, I, 21; Ibn al-Mubârak, *Kitab al-zuhd*, I, 229, 230.

(111) Bukhârî, Adab 24; Tirmidhî, *Birr* 15; Ahmad ibn Hanbal, *al-Musnad*, V, 265.

(112) Ahmad ibn Hanbal, II, 263, 387; al-Bayhaqî, *al-Sunan al-Kubrâ*, IV, 60.

The owner of the orphan is Allah,
So it is a sin to hurt the orphans.
Do not think that an orphan is weak;
His tears are his weapon! (113)

The Prophet's Advice about the Rights of Neighbors

Prophet Muhammad (peace be upon him) urged in his teachings to respect the rights of one's neighbors. In a hadith he has said, "Gabriel repeatedly gave me advice about the rights of the neighbors to such an extent that I was led to conjecture that they will take a share from my legacy when I die" (114).

In another hadith, it is stated that, "Non-Muslim neighbors have one right. Muslim neighbors have two rights. The neighbor who is both a Muslim and a relative has three rights" (115). The rights of the neighbors include not looking at their windows, not disturbing them with the smell of cooking, nor doing an action to them that they dislike.

Abu Dharr al-Ghifari who was from among the poor of the companions said, "The Prophet ordered me to put more water in my meal so that I could offer some to my neighbor" (116). Abu Dharr was among the needy of the companions. Since he did not have extra food, the only way he could increase his meal was by adding extra water to it. This hadith

---

(113) Mehmet Aslan,
(114) Bukhârî, *Adab* 28; Muslim, *Birr* 140; Abû Dâwûd, *Adab* 123; Ibn Mâjah, *Adab* 4; Ahmad ibn Hanbal, *al-Musnad*, II, 85, 160, 259.
(115) Abû Bakr al-Qurashî, *Makârim al-akhlaq*, I, 105; Hannâd al-Kûfî, *al-Zuhd*, II, 504; al-Bayhaqî, *Shu'ab al-Îmân*, VII, 84.
(116) Ibn Mâjah, *At'imah* 58 ; al-Tabarânî, *al-Mu'jam al-Awsat*, IV, 54.

demonstrates that even poverty is not an excuse for not respecting the rights of neighbors.

The following hadith is yet another example of how careful the companions were in respecting the rights of neighbors. Ibn Umar (may Allah be pleased with him) narrated the following event. "There were seven households, all of which were poor. One sent a sheep's head as food to one of the families. The chief of the household thought that his neighbor needed it more and sent it to them. The second neighbor thought the same way and sent it to the third neighbor. The other neighbors also thought the same way and sent the sheep's head to the next neighbor until it eventually returned to the first household." [117]

❦

The mercy of the Messenger of Allah (peace be upon him) extended even to those who had passed away. The most important concern in reference to those who had passed away is the rights of those whom the deceased were unable to pay while they were still alive. The Messenger of Allah (peace be upon him) always asked before funeral prayers if the deceased person had debts. If he or she had unpaid debts, he postponed the funeral prayers until these debts were paid off. [118]

Because he was the Prophet of mercy and compassion, Rasulullah (peace be upon him) was extremely concerned about preventing a person from entering his grave with debts.

---

(117) al-Hâkim, *al-Mustadrak*, II, 526; Ibn Abî Shaybah, *al-Musannaf*, VII, 214; al-Bayhaqî, *Shu'ab al-Îmân*, III, 259 (See also interpret of ayah in the Sûrah of al-Hashr, 59/9).

(118) Ibn Hibbân, *al-Sahîh*, XI, 192; al-Hâkim, *al-Mustadrak*, II, 29.

The Prophet's Conduct with Criminals and Captives of War

In Islam, the cause of a crime is first sought and an extreme effort is made to reform the criminal's personality. Punishment in Islamic law is like the punishment parents give to their children. The purpose of punishing the criminal is not to isolate him but rather to assist him in returning to society.

A poor man called Abbad ibn Shurahbil stole some dates from a garden, putting some of the dates in his pocket. At that time, the owner of the garden caught him and beat him. Abbad, who was very much hurt by the incident, went to the Prophet to complain. Prophet Muhammad (peace be upon him) called the owner of the garden and said to him;

"Do not you know he is uneducated! He does not know what he is doing (Did you give him advice?) Moreover, he was hungry; you should have fed him." [119]. The owner of the garden became so upset with what he did that he gave dates to Abbad along with two sacks of wheat.

These statements are not intended to protect robbers, but rather to cure the social problems giving rise to theft. The Prophet (peace be upon him) stated clearly that he would cut off the hand of his daughter as a punishment if she were to commit burglary.

Prophet Muhammad (peace be upon him) was, in particular, compassionate with captives of war. He said to his companions:

"They are your brothers, offer them what you eat and drink!" [120].

---

(119) Nasâî, *Adab al-qadâ* 21: Abû Dâwûd, *Jihâd* 85.
(120) Muslim, *Aymân* 36-38.

His Behavior towards Enemies and non-Muslims

Abu Basra al-Ghifari, when describing his life prior to entering Islam, commented that, "I came to Medina and was hosted by the Prophet (peace be upon him). On that evening, I drank the milk of seven goats. The Prophet (peace be upon him) did not say anything about my roughness. On that night he went to sleep hungry without showing any sign of displeasure or anger. Witnessing this high morality, I acted more intelligently and embraced Islam..."

Since Prophet Muhammad (peace be upon him) was sent as a mercy to the world, his compassion and care encompass all creatures. One day, they asked him to make a prayer for the condemnation of some enemies. In response, he said, "I was not sent to this world for condemnation; I have been sent as a Prophet of Mercy" (121).

When he went to Taif, the ignorant polytheists and arrogant people of the city stoned him. The Archangel Gabriel came to him and asked, "Shall I bring together these two mountains and destroy the people of Taif who are living in between?" He was not pleased by this suggestion and made a special prayer for this society who stoned him: "O my Lord! Please give right guidance to these people! I ask for a Muslim progeny from their lineage." (122) As a result of his prayer, the people of Taif ultimately accepted Islam.

---

(121) Muslim, *Fadâil* 126; Tirmidhî, *Da'awat* 118.

(122) Bukhârî, *Badul-khalq* 7; Muslim, *Jihâd* 111; Nasâî, *al-Sunan al-Kubrâ*, IV, 405; Ibn Hibbân, *al-Sahîh*, XIV, 516.

The Forgiveness of the Prophet

Allah likes to forgive. He has promised to forgive the sins of humans if they sincerely repent. In the Qur'an, he has also asked his servants to be forgiving because He is oft-forgiving.

The condition for Allah's forgiveness is to feel remorse, to obey the orders of Allah, and to stay away from His prohibitions. The best examples of forgiveness are found in the life of the Prophet (peace be upon him). He forgave Hind, who bit the liver of his uncle Hamza at the Battle of Uhud. During the conquering of Mecca after she became a Muslim, Hind came from behind the Prophet and asked,

"O Messenger of Allah, do you recognize me?"

Prophet Muhammad, five years after Uhud, indicated that he still remembered her scream of happiness after Hamza was martyred.

"How can I forget that scream?"

Yet, he forgave her for the sake of Kalima-i Tawhid which she uttered on entering Islam.

On the other hand, Prophet Muhammad said to the people of Mecca who were waiting with great anxiety after being conquered:

"– O, Community of Quraysh! What do you expect that I will do to you?"

The Qurayshites said,

"We expect that you will forgive us. Your are a brother filled with kindness and mercy. You are also the son of a brother who had kindness and mercy..."

Thereupon, the Prophet (peace be upon him) said,

"I say to you what Prophet Joseph said to his brothers: "This day, no reproach be (cast) on you; may Allah forgive you; you may go; you are free." [123]

In another address, he said, "Today is the day of mercy. Today is the day Allah increased the power of Islam by the Qurayshites."

One of the fiercest enemies of Islam in Mecca was Abu Jahl, which literally means "father of ignorance." His son Ikrima was also a leading enemy of Islam. Ikrima escaped to Yemen when Mecca was conquered. His wife became a Muslim and later brought him to the presence of the Prophet (peace be upon him), who met him with pleasure and said to him:

"O the running cavalry! Welcome!" He forgave him without even reminding him of his wrongdoings against Muslims. [124]

Habir ibn Aswad was yet another enemy of Islam. During the migration of the Prophet's daughter Zainab from Mecca to Medina, he intentionally kicked her while she was riding a camel and caused her to fall to the ground. She was pregnant at the time. She was heavily injured and lost the baby. Habir ibn Asad committed many other crimes like that. After Mecca was conquered he wanted to escape but could not. He accepted Islam and came to the presence of the Prophet (peace be upon him) who then forgave him. [125]

---

(123) Nasâî, *al-Sunan al-Kubrâ*, VI, 382; al-Bayhaqî, *al-Sunan al-Kubrâ*, IX, 118; al-Rabi' ibn Habîb, *Musnad al-Rabi'*, I, 170; Tahâwî, *Sharh Ma'ânî al-Âthâr*, III, 325.

(124) Ibn Hagar al-'Asqalânî, *al-Isâbah*, IV, 538.

(125) Ibn Hagar al-'Asqalânî, *al-Isâbah*, VI, 524-527; Ibn AbdilBarr, *al-Isîi'âb*, IV, 1536.

The Prophet (peace be upon him) frequently said, "O my Lord! Forgive my people for they know not!" [126].

A man called Hamamah accepted Islam and cut his relations with the polytheist Meccans. The Meccans were shocked by his decision and approached the Prophet to ask the man to maintain his trade with them. The Prophet (peace be upon him) sent Hamamah a letter and asked him to continue his trade with the Quraysh. Although the polytheists had held the Muslims under siege for three years and had tortured them by letting them remain hungry, the Messenger of Allah (peace be upon him) nevertheless forgave them. They all became Muslims when confronted with such endless forgiveness.

One day, a group of eighty people came to kill the Prophet (peace be upon him), but all of them were caught. The Messenger of Allah (peace be upon him), forgave each of them as well.

After Khaybar was conquered, a woman offered a poisoned meal to the Prophet (peace be upon him), who noticed the poison after the first bite. The Jewish woman confessed her plot but the Prophet forgave her [127]. In the Qur'an, it is stated that one should *"Hold to forgiveness; command what is right; but turn away from the ignorant"* (Qur'an, Araf, 7/199).

❀

The Prophet (peace be upon him) represented to perfection the best behavior for humans with his sincere, simple and humble conduct with people. His conduct did

---

(126) Ibn Mâjah, *Manâsik* 56; Ahmad ibn Hanbal, *al-Musnad*, IV, 14.
(127) Bukhârî, *Tıbb* 55; Muslim, *Selam* 43; Abû Dâwûd, *Diyat* 6; Ibn Mâjah, *Tıbb* 45; Dârimî, *Muqaddimah* 11; Ahmad ibn Hanbal, *al-Musnad*, II, 451.

not emanate from him superficially or unintentionally, but rather emerged from the depth of his soul.

Adiyy ibn Khatim told the following story:

There was a time, when I had not embraced Islam. I went to visit the Prophet (peace be upon him). He invited me to his home. On the way, an old woman stopped him. The Messenger of Allah waited for a long time until the woman had finished what she had to say. I said to myself, "By God! He is not a king."

Then we went to his home. He gave me a mat made from skin filled with dry leaves and said to me:

"Please sit on this."

I insisted:

"Please you sit on it."

But he repeated:

"You sit!"

I sat on the mat because I did not want to refuse his offer. He sat on the ground. This time, I said to myself:

"By God! This is not something a king can do."

Then we started conversing. Prophet Muhammad (peace be upon him) told me that I belonged to the Rakusi [128] sect, and although it was forbidden according to my faith, I collected one forth of the people's income as taxes. I was shocked. Immediately, I realized that he was a Prophet because he knew hidden secrets. [129]

---

(128) A sect which was composed of elements from Christianity and the Sabii religion.

(129) Ibn Hishâm, *al-Sirah al-Nabawiyyahh*, II, 580; Ahmad ibn Hanbal, *al-*

All these incidents display with extreme clarity the high character of the Prophet.

❀

Prophet Muhammad was a living example of the moral principles expressed in the Qur'an. He forgave all the wrong done against him. Yet, as far as the crimes committed against the members of public were concerned, he acted with utmost objevtivity and care to fulfil the orders of Allah. Usamah, an outstanding Companion, interceded on behalf of a woman who committed theft. The woman was from a noble family. Usamah asked him to forgive her. The color of the Prophet (peace be upon him) faded out of sadness and he responded with a dire voice, "I would cut off the hand of even my own daughter Fatima in order to punish her in the event she became involved in theft" [130]

The Generosity of the Prophet

Ibn Abbas, (may Allah be pleased with him), related the generosity of the Prophet (peace be upon him) as follows: "The Messenger of Allah was the most generous of all people. His generosity increased more in Ramadan. He never said "no" to someone who asked for something from him!" [131].

Musnad, IV, 379; al-Tabarânî, al-Mu'jam al-Awsat, VI, 360; Ibn Abî Shaybah, al-Musannaf, VII, 342.

(130) Bukhârî, Hudûd 12; Muslim, Hudûd 9; Nasâî, Kat'us-sariq12; Abû Dâwûd, Hudûd 4; Ibn Mâjah, Hudûd 6; Dârimî, Hudûd 5; Ahmad ibn Hanbal, al-Musnad, VI, 162.

(131) Bukhârî, Bad' al-wahy 5-6; Nasâî, Siyâm 2; Ahmad ibn Hanbal, al-Musnad, I, 288, 363; Ibn Hibbân, al-Sahîh, VIII, 225.

One of the most beautiful characteristics of the Prophet was to refrain from denying someone who asked for something. In the event there was nothing to offer, he smiled in order to make him happy. The following incident is an excellent example:

The Prophet described himself only as an officer of distribution and he stressed that everything was provided by Allah. One day a man came to the Prophet (peace be upon him). When he saw the goats of the Prophet, he asked for a goat. The Messenger of Allah (peace be upon him) gave him all his goats. When the man returned to his tribe he told them the following: "Muhammad is so generous that he is not afraid of poverty!"[132]

Another person came to visit the Prophet (peace be upon him) and asked for something. The Prophet (peace be upon him) did not have anything to give to him. He suggested that the man get a loan and promised him that he would pay the loan on the man's behalf.

Similar to his ancestor Abraham (peace be upon him), he never had a meal by himself without guests. He used to pay the debts of the dead or had others pay. He did not offer funeral prayers before closing the debt. He said:

"A generous person is close to Allah, to Paradise and to the people; but he is seperated from the Hellfire. To the contrary a stingy person is seperated from Allah, from Paradise and from the people while he is close to the Hellfire" [133].

(132) Muslim, *Fadâil* 57; Ahmad ibn Hanbal, *al-Musnad*, III, 107, 259; Ibn Hibbân, *al-Sahîh*, X, 354; Ibn Khuzaymah, *al-Sahîh*, IV, 70;

(133) Tirmidhî, *Birr* 40; al-Tabarânî, *al-Mu'jam al-Awsat*, III, 27; al-Ismâilî, *Mu'jam*, III, 733; al-Bayhaqî, *Shu'ab al-Îmân*, VII, 428, 429.

In another hadith, he is reported to have said, "A true Believer is never characterized by the following two qualities: stinginess or immorality" [134].

The Generosity of the Companions

The companions competed with each other to emulate the example of the Prophet (peace be upon him). The following examples illustrate this race for virtue.

Umar (may Allah be pleased with him) told the following story.

"One day, the Prophet (peace be upon him) commanded us to give charity. At that time, I had some money with me. I thought to myself that this was the day to pass Abu Bakr in good deeds and presented half of my money to the Prophet. The Messenger of Allah (peace be upon him) asked,

"What did you leave to your family?"

In response, I said:

"The same amount I brought to you."

Then, Abu Bakr came. He brought all his money. Rasulullah (peace be upon him) asked him, "O Abu Bakr! What did you leave for your family?"

He responded by saying, "I left them Allah and the Prophet!"

After hearing his answer, I said to myself, "I will never be able to pass Abu Bakr, (may Allah be pleased with him), in any matter." [135]

---

(134) Tirmidhî, *Birr* 41; al-Tayalisi, *al-Musnad*, I, 293; al-Qudâî, *Musnad al-Shihâb*, I , 211.

(135) Tirmidhî, *Manâqıb* 16; Abû Dâwûd, *Zakât* 40; Dârimî, *Zakât* 26; Al-

Abu Bakr and Umar (may Allah be pleased with them) were perfect heirs to the Prophet (peace be upon him) in refusing to incline towards luxury and the splendor of this world. Their life style surprised the emperors of Iran and Byzantium.

No doubt, their good conduct was also reflected in the life of other companions as well. For instance, one day, a beggar came to Ali (may Allah be pleased with him) and asked for something. Ali said to his sons Hasan and Husayn;

"Go to your mother and bring the six dirhams we have." They went home and brought the six dirhams they had and gave them to their father who in turn gave them to the beggar. Yet, at the time, they needed that money. Fatima had been planning to buy flour with that money.

Ali (may Allah be pleased with him) returned home. Immediately after he stepped into his house, a man who had wanted to sell his camel arrived. He said he wanted to sell his camel for forty dirhams and was ready to receive the payment later. He tied the camel in the garden and went on. Soon after, a man appeared and expressed his willingness to buy the camel for two hundred dirhams. He instantly paid the money and left with the camel.

Ali gave forty dirhams to the first owner of the camel and the rest of the money to Fatima. He also said to her, "This is the promise of Allah through his Prophet. "Whoever does a good deed, he will receive ten times its value as reward." We gave ten dirhams and Allah gave us back ten times more."

Hâkim, *al-Mustadrak*, I, 574; al-Bayhaqî, *al-Sunan*, IV, 180; al-Bazzâr, *al-Musnad*, I, 263, 394.

The following incident which was related by Huzayfa is significant, for it reflects the altruism of the companions.

During the battle of Yarmuk when the intensity of the conflict subsided, and the injured Muslims were dying on the extremely hot sand; I recollected my energy and started to look for Harith, my uncle's son. After walking among the wounded soldiers who were taking their last breaths, I found him. Unfortunately, Harith was in a sea of blood and could barely speak even with the movement of his eyes. I showed him the leather water-bottle which I carried and asked him, "Do you want some water?"

His lips were dry from the hot weather and probably he wished to have some water. It seemed as if he was trying to tell me his painful situation by the movement of his eyes. I opened the leather water-bottle and was ready to give him some water. Suddenly Ikrima's voice was heard in the distance. "Water!... Water!... Please a drop of water!.."

When the son of my uncle heard this cry, he indicated with the movements of his eyes to take the water to him. I rushed to Ikrima bypassing the martyrs who were lying in the hot sand. Finally, I reached Ikrima and was ready to place the bottle of water in his hand. Suddenly, we heard the moaning of Iyash.

"Please give me a drop of water! For God's sake, a drop of water!"

When Ikrima heard his cry for water, he indicated with the movement of his hand to take the water to Iyash. Like Harith, he had refused to drink. When I found Iyash after searching for him among the wounded martyrs, I heard his last words. He was saying,

"O Allah! We have not spared our lives in the cause of faith. Do not spare from us the level of martyrdom. Forgive our mistakes!"

He was about to become a martyr. He saw the water bottle I brought but he did not have time to drink because he could barely finish uttering the *Kalima-i Shahadah* (The formula which states: I bear witness that there is no deity but Allah; I also bear witness that Muhammad is His servant and messenger).

I ran back immediately to Ikrima and while trying to offer him water, I realized that he became a martyr. I thought to return to the son of my uncle, Harith. I ran to him. Unfortunately, his soul also returned to Allah while lying on the fiery sand. Painfully, a bottle of water had been left full among the three martyrs.

Huzayfa (may Allah be pleased with him) related his state of mind at the time as follows: "I came across many incidents in my life, but none of them influenced me as much as this event. Their extremely altruistic, caring and compassionate relationship, although they were not the relatives of each other, left deep traces of admiration in my memory. [136]

The Prophet's Sincerity, Honesty and Integrity

The Messenger of Allah felt extreme pity for people who did not know what was right from what was wrong, the

---

(136) al-Hâkim, *al-Mustadrak*, III, 270; al-Tabarânî, *al-Mu'jam al-Kabîr*, III, 259; al-Mizzi, *Tahthib al-Kamâl*, V, 301; Ibn al-Mubârak, *al-Zuhd*, I, 185; al-Qurtubî, *Tafsîr*, XVIII, 28.

orders and prohibitions of Allah. As he went from door to door to teach the religion of Allah, at times, the doors were shut in his face. Yet he did not feel resent this misbehavior against him as much as he felt sorrow for people's ignorance.

To these people, he said, *"No reward do I ask of you for this (Qur'an); Nor am I a pretender!"* (Qur'an, Sad, 38/86).

No one reached the level of honesty and integrity practiced by the Prophet (peace be upon him). He was an orphan. He was introduced to trade by his uncle Abu Talib. His honesty and integrity were acknowledged by everyone, which earned him the honorary title, al-Amin, the trustworthy. Everyone in the community both poor and rich alike called him al-Amin. The noble woman of Mecca, Khadija, admired his honesty and asked his hand in marriage. Our mother Khadija later served as his most vital supporter. When the first revelation came, she offered moral support to the Prophet (peace be upon him). She always stood at his side and comforted him during dangerous times.

Rasulullah (peace be upon him) led a pure life. Even those who refused to accept his message out of arrogance, acknowledged his good qualities.

Since Islam first emerged fourteen centuries ago, there is no one who has not acknowledged his integrity and his heart. Even those in the Jewish community, who had been the enemies of Islam, came to him when they had a disagreement among themselves. Rasullullah (peace be upon him) solved their conflicts. He was just and fair towards Christians and Jews, alike.

He gave the following advice to Ali about justice:

"Never judge prior to listening to both parties! You can give a correct judgement only after listening to both sides!" [137]

When the Prophet (peace be upon him) decided to immigrate from Mecca to Medina, he made Ali his deputy to return the jewelry that had been entrusted to him. [138]

The Bashfulness of the Prophet

According to the description of his companions, the Prophet (peace be upon him) was more bashful than a young girl covering herself from unwanted eyes. He never spoke with a loud voice. When he passed by others, he used to do so slowly and with a smile on his face. When he heard displeasing talk, he never said anything in front of the people. Nevertheless, his face reflected his feelings and his thoughts. Thus, people around him were very careful about their conduct when they were near him. He never laughed loudly because of his modesty. The most he did was only to smile. In a hadith it is stated that,

"Bashfulness is from faith. Bashful people will be in Paradise! Shamelessness arises from the hardness of heart. Those with hardened hearts will go to the Hellfire" [139].

Another hadith states:

"Faith and modesty are together. When one leaves, the other departs, too." [140].

---

(137) Ahmad ibn Hanbal, *al-Musnad*, I, 90.

(138) Ibn Hishâm, *al-Sirah al-Nabawiyyahh*, I, 482; Ibn al-Kathir, *al-Bidâyah van-nihâyah*, II, 176.

(139) Bukhârî, *Îmân* 16; Muslim, *Îmân* 57-59; Abû Dâwûd, *Sunnah* 14; Tirmidhî, *Îmân* 7; Nasâî, *Îmân* 16; Ibn Mâjah, *Zuhd* 17; Muwatta, *Husn al-Khuluq* 10; Ahmad ibn Hanbal, *al-Musnad*, II, 56, 147.

(140) al-Tabarânî, *al-Mu'jam al-Awsat*, VIII, 174 and same book IV, 374; al-

"Rude talk does not bring anything except shame! Modesty and decency decorate wherever they may be" [141].

Real modesty is gained by "remembering death" which is a means for the removal, from the heart, of love for this world. Prophet Muhammad (peace be upon him) continuously advised his companions to extend to Allah the profound respect He deserves. Once, they said that they thanked Allah modestly. The Prophet (peace be upon him) explained that real modesty involves cleaning all one's organs from prohibited actions and remembering death. Next, he stated that only those who truly desire the next world abandon their love for this world. And, only they show true modesty of conduct towards Allah [142].

The Altruism of the Prophet

Prophet Muhammad (peace be upon him) not only felt sorry for the suffering of the people, but he painstakingly worked for their success. This quality is mentioned in the Qur'an.

"Now has come unto you a Messenger from amongst yourselves; it grieves him that you should suffer; ardently anxious is he over you; to the Believers is he most kind and merciful" (Qur'an, Tawba, 9/128). In this verse, Allah the Most High honored his Messenger by assigning him two of His own attributes, Rauf and Rahim, meaning most kind and merciful respectively.

Bayhaqî, *Shu'ab al-Îmân*, VI, 140.
(141) Muslim, *Birr* 78; Abû Dâwûd, *Jihâd* 1.
(142) Tirmidhî, *Sifatu'l-Qiyamah* 24; Ahmad ibn Hanbal, *al-Musnad*, I, 387; al-Hâkim, *al-Mustadrak*, IV, 359; Ibn Abî Shaybah, *al-Musannaf*, VII, 77; al-Tabarânî, *al-Mu'jam al-Awsat*, VII, 226.

He always struggled for the success of his people and he was happy and tranquil whenever he saw them making progress towards their own self-improvement and integrity.

He was not like any other leader who wished good for his community. On the contrary, he was a guide who supported his community with all the means at his disposal. Once a Companion asked how to decide whether his condition was good or bad. The Messenger of Allah (peace be upon him) told him the following:

"Whoever aims to gain a worldly profit through worship, which is normally performed for reward in Paradise, will achieve nothing in the Hereafter" [143]

He was a Mercy, embracing all of humanity with his actions, speeches and morality. He was their guide. He faced the most challenging difficulties and trials in the cause of true religion. He fulfilled the divine task he was assigned in a perfect way. He was so anxious and patient in doing so, that at times, revelation came to warn him not to let himself perish on this path.

The high level of virtue displayed by the Prophet (peace be upon him) for the happiness of humanity is expressed in the following verse in the Qur'an. *"It may be you will kill yourself with grief, that they do not become Believers"* (Qur'an, Shu'ara, 42/3).

This verse demonstrates that the Prophet (peace be upon

(143) Ahmad b. Hanbal, *al-Musnad*, V, 134; Ibn Hibbân, *al-Sahîh*, II, 32; al-Hâkim, *al-Mustadrak*, IV, 346; al-Bayhaqî, *Shu'ab al-Îmân*, V, 334.

him) wanted, out of his mercy and compassion, that all humanity believe in Allah, and thus save themselves from the Hellfire.

When Hamza heard that Abu Jahl attacked the Prophet (peace be upon him), he also attacked Abu Jahl, and said to the Prophet, "O Muhammad! Be happy! I took your revenge from Abu Jahl..." Rasulullah (peace be upon him) said to him:

"I have nothing to do with revenge! I will be happy if you accept Islam." Hamza realized the wisdom in the answer and embraced Islam. [144]

His noble conduct and sublime morality had nothing to do with personal gain, materialistic motives nor with the feeling of revenge. On examination we may see that the Prophet (peace be upon him) never took revenge in his entire life. [145]

Prophet Muhammad (peace be upon him) never openly corrected a companion for a mistake he made. Instead he used to say, "What is happening to me that I see you doing like that!" [146]

He attributed errors of vision to himself without attributing the mistake to the person he was talking to. Prophet Muhammad (peace be upon him), who took extraordinary measures to avoid breaking the heart of his

(144) Ibn Hishâm, *al-Sirah al-Nabawiyyahh*, I, 292; al-Hâkim, *al-Mustadrak*, III, 213; al-Tabarânî, *al-Mu'jam al-Kabîr*, III, 139; Ibn al-Kathîr, *al-Bidâyah van-nihâyah*, II, 32.

(145) al-Bukhârî, *Manâqib* 23; Muslim, *Fadâil* 77; Abû Dâwûd, *Adab* 4; Muwatta, *Husnul-khuluq* 2; Ahmad ibn Hanbal, *al-Musnad*, V, 130, 223.

(146) Bukhârî, *Aymân* 3; Ibn Hibbân, *al-Sahîh*, IV, 534; al-Hâkim, *al-Mustadrak*, II, 515.

companions, was a monument of mercy. These qualities were reflected both in his deeds and in his speeches. As an example let us contemplate on the following speech:

"O Believers! May Allah keep you secure! May He watch after you! May He protect you! May He help you! May He elevate you! May He guide you! May He keep you under his own guard! May he keep you away from all sorts of bad luck! And May He protect your religion for you!" [147]

The Prophet (peace be upon him) was sent as a mercy to the worlds. He was a manifestation of the Divine Names, al-Ghafur and al-Rahman, that is the Most Forgiving and the Most Compassionate. He felt sorry for people who denied his message and prayed that they would be saved from the Hellfire. As a result, a divine warning came:

"Yet it may be, if they believe not in this statement, that thou (Muhammad) wilt torment thy soul with grief over their footsteps." (Qur'an, Kahf, 18/6).

His companions spread with love and joy to remote areas the knowledge, blessings, virtue and spiritual qualities gained through association with him. This was an example of the principle of "love the creature for the sake of the Creator."

Everyone was granted a share of his high character and generosity. His benevolence and mercy were like a great river which spread over and fed all lands without discrimination. No one was left hungry, thirsty or alone while around him.

---

(147) al-Bazzâr, *al-Musnad*, V, 395; al-Tabarânî, *al-Mu'jam al-Awsat*, IV, 208; Abû Nu'aym al-Isbahânî, *Hilyah al-Awliyâ*, IV, 168; al-Bağdâdî, *Muwaddıh*, II, 147.

His Loyalty

Keeping a promise is a means for the attainment of salvation from the Hellfire; it is also a quality of Prophets and virtuous people. With this quality, life acquires direction and order. It is a measure of humanity and a criterion for judging individuals and nations. People attain happiness to the extent that they respect it.

Living at zenith of loyalty, the Prophet (peace be upon him) served in this regard as a perfect example for humanity. Regarding this, Aishah reiterated the following story.

"Once an old woman came to visit the Prophet (peace be upon him). They had a warm conversation. After the old woman left, I asked him:

"O Rasulullah! You showed so much interest to that old woman! I am curious about who she was?" He said, "She is someone who used to visit us when Khadija was alive. Know that "loyalty comes from faith." (148).

A group came to the Prophet (peace be upon him) after the incident of Hunayn. They wanted freedom for the captives of war. One of them said, "O Muhammad! Our tribe has your milk mothers and milk sisters!"

The Messenger of Allah (peace be upon him) responded with great loyalty, "I free all the captives that belong to me and the sons of Abdulmuttalib."

The Immigrants and the Helpers who saw this refined behavior followed his action by saying, "We also free our captives for the sake of the Prophet!"

---

(148) al-Hâkim, *al-Mustadrak,* I, 62; al-Qudâî, *Musnad al-Shihâb,* II, 102; al-Bayhaqî, *Shu'ab al-Îmân,* VI, 517.

As a result, on that day, thousands of captives were freed without any ransom [149]. This was a gesture of gratitude and the loyalty to the milk he had been given as a child. It is an excellent lesson for an oppressive nation. Unfortunately, humans quickly forget the favors whose traces fade in the memory. Usually, "LOYALTY" exists only as a word in the dictionary.

During his terminal illness, the Prophet (peace be upon him) came to the Masjid, went up to the pulpit, and said, "O Immigrants! Treat the Helpers kindly because the population is increasing but their number is still the same: They have served as a shelter for me. Treat the good ones among them with goodness, and forgive the mistakes of the wrongdoers."

The loyalty the Prophet displayed to the Helpers for the favors he received, is an excellent example for all of us. His life is full of many examples of loyalty. For instance, before the Hijrah, while his enemies were planning how to kill him, he was planning how to return the jewelry entrusted to him.

On the day of Uhud, he had two companions who were good friends in life buried in the same grave and then said, "This is because they were sincere friends in this world." [150].

The matchless morality of the Prophet (peace be upon him) was reflected in the lives and relations of his companions, based on the love they had for one another. Uthman was sent to Mecca on the day of Hudaybiya. He told

---

(149) Bukhârî, *al-Târikh al-sagîr*, I, 5; al-Tabarânî, *al-Mu'jam al-Kabîr*, V, 271; Abû Bakr al-Qurashî, *Makârim al-akhlâq*, I, 116.
(150) Ibn Abi Shaybah, *al-Musannaf*, VII, 367; Ahmad b. Hanbal, *al-Musnad*, V, 299; Ibn Hishâm, *al-Sirah al-Nabawiyyahh*, II, 98.

159

the polytheists in Mecca that the Prophet (peace be upon him) came only to make pilgrimage to the Kaba. They refused this appeal but agreed to allowed only Uthman to make the pilgrimage. However, Uthman (may Allah be pleased with him) rejected this offer and said:

"I cannot perform the pilgrimage if the Prophet is not allowed to do so!.. I cannot stay where the Prophet is not accepted..."

Exactly at this time, the Prophet was accepting the bay'ah of the companions. Since Uthman was not there, in his place, the Prophet (peace be upon him) put one of his hands over the other and said:

"O my Lord! This bay'ah is for Uthman! Verily, he is a servant of your Messenger." [151]

In essence, becoming a true believer is a function of the degree to which we are able to emulate the example of the Prophet.

❀

Prophet Muhammad was a vehicle for many miracles. Also, he assisted humans in the cultivation of their personalities. New qualities were thus infused into the community which would bring beauty and honor to culture and civilization. This revolutionary change in the character of humans under the guidance of Prophet Muhammad is an immense miracle. Good words, refined behavior and

---

(151) Ahmad b. Hanbal, *al-Musnad*, IV, 324; Ibn Abdilbarr, *al-Tamhîd*, XII, 148; Ibn Hishâm, *al-Sîrah al-Nabawiyyah*, II, 315; Ibnul-Kathîr, *al-Bidayah wan-Nihayah*, II, 169.

exemplary actions served as causes for this enrichment of civilization. At the origin of all, stands the exemplary actions, speeches and practices of the Prophet (peace be upon him).

In the balance he established between opposite aspects of life, no shortcoming remained. For instance, he balanced work for this world with work for the Hereafter. Likewise, he balanced ascetic tendencies with those directed toward the satisfaction of desires. It is impossible to find another personality, in the entirety of human history, comparable to him.

In social history, it is possible to encounter great figures who had outstanding abilities in different fields of life. Generally, their abilities are only limited to one field. The personality of the Prophet (peace be upon him) however, included outstanding qualities in all realms of life.

The following moral principles, which were set by the Prophet (peace be upon him) expess the higher standard of his life. According to the Prophet (peace be upon him),

"My Lord commanded nine things:

1. Fear Allah whether you are alone or in the crowd.

2. Be just and fair whether you are pleased or angry.

3. Live moderately whether you are rich or poor.

4. Maintain your relations with your relatives even if they don't do so.

5. Give to the one who deprives you.

6. Forgive the one who wrongs you.

7. Contemplate while you are silent.

8. Mention Allah when you speak.

9. Take lessons when you look." [152]

On his sword, the following was written: "Forgive the one who wronged you; help your relatives even if they do not care about you; respond with goodness to the one who harmed you; say the truth even if it is against your interest." [153]

Huzayfa (may Allah be pleased with him) narrated that the Prophet (peace be upon him) said:

"None of you should be a parasite. One type of individual says "My reactions depend on those around me. If they treat me nicely, I also treat them nicely; if they mistreat me, I mistreat them as well. Instead, you should take the following as your principle. When they treat you nicely, you also treat them nicely; when they mistreat you, you do not act as they have." [154]

He also said, "Allah dislikes three things for you:

1. Gossiping,

2. Being a spendthrift,

3. Questioning unnecessarily." [155]

---

(152) Nasâî, *Sahw* 62; Ahmad ibn Hanbal, *al-Musnad*, IV, 148; *Ibn Abî Shaybah, al-Musannaf*, VI, 45; al-Tabarânî, *al-Mu'jam al-Awsat*, V, 328.

(153) Ahmad ibn Hanbal, *al-Musnad*, IV, 148; al-Hâkim, *al-Mustadrak*, II, 563; al-Tabarânî, *al-Mu'jam al-Kabîr*, XVII, 269; al-Bayhaqî, *al-Sunan al-Kubrâ*, X, 235.

(154) Tirmidhî, *Birr* 62; (Some version of this hadith was narrated from ·Abdullah ibn Mas'ûd as *mawkûf hadith* for example; al-Tabarânî, *al-Mu'jam al-Kabîr*, IX , 152; Abû Nu'aym al-Isbahânî, *Hilyah al-Awliyâ*, I, 137; Ibn al-Jawzî, *Safvatus-safvah*, I, 421).

(155) ·Bukhârî, *Zakât* 53; Muslim, *Akdiyah* 12, 13; Ahmad ibn Hanbal, *al-Musnad*, II, 327, 360; Ibn Khuzaymah, *al-Sahîh*, I, 104.

Other advise of the Prophet (peace be upon him) includes, "Do not laugh at your brother's trouble because Allah, the Most High, may save him from that trouble and put you in his place." [156]

Those who study the life of Prophet Muhammad (peace be upon him) will see that he has always been the Prophet of mercy and compassion. He never condemned anyone and raised excellent people in an oppressive society. For example, the only thing he did, when he was stoned in Taif, was to ask Allah to give them guidance. [157] When he entered the Kaba, after ten years of adversity arising from the people of Mecca, he showed humbleness and tolerance. He did not even take the key of the Kaba from Uthman ibn Talha who had had it for a long time. He said, "Today is the day of kindness and loyalty." [158]

He is the only sultan who did not leave an heir in his place. He said, "We, the Prophets, do not bequeath; whatever we leave is charity for all Muslims."[159] The only legacy he left for his Ummah was his perfect example.

(156) Tirmidhî, *Qıyâmah* 54; al-Tabarânî, *al-Mu'jam al-Awsat*, IV, 111; al-Qudâî, *Musnad al-Shihâb*, II, 77; al-Bayhaqî, *Shu'ab al-Îmân*, V, 315.

(157) Bukhârî, *Bad al-khalq* 7; Muslim, *Jihâd* 111; Nasâî, *al-Sunan al-Kubrâ*, IV, 405; Ibn Hibbân, *al-Sahîh*, XIV, 516.

(158) Ibn Hishâm, *al-Sirah al-Nabawiyyahh*, II, 412; Ibn Kathîr, *al-Bidayah wan-Nihayah*, II, 300.

(159) Bukhârî, *Khumus* 1; Muslim, *Jihâd* 54; Abû Dâwûd, *İmârah* 19; Tirmidhî, *Siyar* 44; Nasâî, *Fay'* 9; Muwatta, *Kalâm* 27; Ahmad ibn Hanbal, *al-Musnad*, I, 4.

CONCLUSION

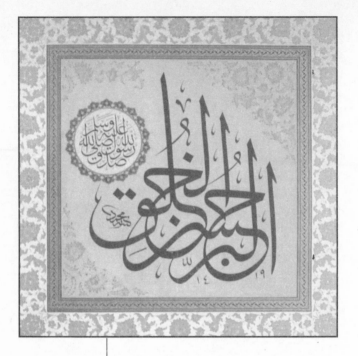

"Piety is kindness." **(Hadith, Bukhari, Muslim, Tirmidhi)**

$\mathcal{I}$n creation, only humans have a share in all the attributes of Allah–with the exception of eternity. Along with this, as a result of His wisdom, Allah equipped humans with the potential for righteousness and corruption. He, thus, made humans capable of benevolence and evil.

From this perspective, the purpose of religion is to restrain the animal desires of the human soul, while raising to perfection the good qualities. Yet, for this goal to be realized, humanity needs a perfect as well as a concrete example to emulate. One of the reasons prophets have been sent is to meet this need for a perfect example for humanity to follow.

Allah, the Most High, says in the Qur'an: *"We sent not a Messenger, but to be obeyed, in accordance with the leave of Allah..."* (Qur'an, Nisa, 4/64).

This quality reached its peak in Prophet Muhammad, (peace be upon him), which is well illustrated in the following verse of the Qur'an: *"You have indeed in the Messenger of Allah an excellent example for those whose hope is in Allah and in the Final Day, and who frequently remember Him"* (Qur'an, Ahzab, 33/21).

The only prophet in history whose life is recorded in the most minute detail is Prophet Muhammad (peace be upon him). His words, deeds and feelings, which have been ceaselessly recorded, have taken their place in history as pages of great honor and significance. His life will serve as an example to humanity until the last day. The following verse bears witness to this fact: *"And surely you have sublime morals"* (Qur'an, Qalam, 68/4).

The blessed personality and life of the Messenger of Allah (peace be upon him), constitute that matchless zenith of perfect human conduct, needed for the spiritual fulfillment of humanity. Allah, the Most High, created him for this purpose for all people. For this reason, He had him pass through all situations in life from being a powerless orphan to being prophet and president of state. The wisdom behind this life path is that all people, regardless of their place in life, can find for themselves an ideal example of conduct for application in their lives to the extent of their ability and power.

The Messenger of Allah (peace be upon him), with his outstanding personality, was chosen as the last prophet for all humanity. Prophet Abraham (peace be upon him) prayed to Allah that Prophet Muhammad might come from his progeny. Prophet Jesus (peace be upon him) gave good tidings of his coming, and the Prophet's mother, Aminah, saw him in a dream before his birth. He was raised directly under the supervision of Allah, ornamented by the most beautiful traits of high character and chosen as the most trustworthy guide for humanity.

It is thus necessary for humanity in these times to follow the example of Prophet Muhammad (peace be upon him) to obtain happiness in this world and the Hereafter. Even attaining the love of Allah depends on following him, as Allah the Most High has explained in the following verse: *"Say "if you do love Allah, follow me; Allah will love you and forgive your sins for Allah is Oft-Forgiving, Most Merciful"* (Qur'an, Al-i Imran, 3/31).

Based on this fact, only those fortunate souls who adopt and internalize the example of the Prophet (peace be upon him) can earn the sublime love of Allah.

The first and the most important outcome of loyalty to the Messenger of Allah (peace be upon him), is to learn the love of Allah. Furthermore, following in the footsteps of the best example of morality and conduct results in sharing in his perfection. Since his is the best morality and conduct, those who believe in him and love him will also become excellent. The inner worlds of those who love him reach to higher levels, even higher than the angels. Their family lives reflect life in Paradise. A society based on his example gains peace and tranquility with breezes blowing through it from the Age of Happiness (asr al-sa'adah). They taste the authentic joy of closeness to Allah in their worship. If everyone, whether rich or poor, supervisor or subordinate, ruler or ruled, strong or weak, was to live as a servant of Allah implementing His orders, this would eventually bring about an exceptional balance in society.

For instance, when the Messenger of Allah (peace be upon him), was given the duty of guiding mankind, many who led immoral and shameful lives, became outstandingly virtuous and exceptional personalities through their new education. Consequently, an evil period ended and a new righteous period began. Slaves gained the dignity and honor of being human; many rulers became just and virtuous through learning about how to be a servant of Allah. The words of Najashi, then the Christian king of Abyssinia, are significant.

"I bear witness that Muhammad is the Messenger of Allah. He is the one whose coming had been foretold by Jesus (peace be upon him). I would go and carry his shoes if I did not have the responsibilities I currently have towards my people [1].

As people saw the happiness and salvation in both worlds offered to them, they rushed to him as a river rushes to sea. This was a gift from Allah, as explained in the following verse of the Qur'an.

"When comes the Help of Allah, and Victory, And thou dost see the people enter Allah's Religion in crowds, Celebrate the praises of thy Lord, and pray for His Forgiveness: For He is Oft-Returning (in Grace and Mercy)." (Qur'an, Nasr, 110/1-3).

Those who followed his path led righteous, decent, peaceful and blessed lives even when facing challenges and difficulties. They became like roses growing among countless wild bushes... Their happiness in the Hereafter is to be even greater. This is because there the Great Intercession (Shafa'ah 'Uzmaa) of the Messenger of Allah will take place on behalf

---

(1) Abû Dâwûd, *Janâiz* 62; Ahmad ibn Hanbal, *al-Musnad*, I, 461; Abû 'Uthman al-Khorasânî, *Kitâb al-Sunan*, II, 228.

of the sinners from the followers of the previous prophets as well as those sinners from his own community, the Ummah. The following hadith explains how this event is to unfold:

I will be the first one to be resurrected among people. When humanity comes to the Divine presence, I will be their spokesman. As they lose hope of the mercy and forgiveness of Allah, I will give them good tidings. I will carry the Banner of Praise (liva al-hamd). I am the most blessed human to approach Allah, yet I do not express this out of self-pride [2].

The Prophet of Mercy will intercede for the sinners on the Day of Judgement and his intercession will be accepted by Allah. The following Qur'anic verse demonstrates that his intercession on behalf of believers is to be accepted by Allah:

"If they had only, when they were unjust to themselves, come unto thee and asked Allah's forgiveness, and the Messenger had asked forgiveness for them, they would have found Allah indeed Oft-returning, Most Merciful." (Qur'an, Nisa, 4/64).

This verse is a divine statement carrying the promise and good tidings that the intercession of the Messenger of Allah (peace be upon him) for his community, (the Ummah) will be accepted by Allah.

The following is another exceptionally good tiding from the Messenger of Allah (peace be upon him):

"On the Day of Judgement, all of humanity will be in a state of shock. They will go to Adam (peace be upon him) to seek help and will say to him,

---

(2) Tirmidhî, *Manâqıb* 1; İbn Mace, *Zuhd* 37; Dârimî, *Muqaddimah* 8; Ahmad b. Hanbal, *al-Musnad*, I, 281; al-Hâkim, *al-Mustadrak*, I, 83; Ibn Hibbân, *al-Sahîh, al-Sahîh*, XIV, 398.

– Please intercede on our behalf in the Divine Presence!

He will tell them:

– I am not in a position to intercede; you should go to Abraham! He is a close friend of the Most Merciful (Khalil al-Rahman)…

People will proceed to Abraham (peace be upon him) and will request him to intercede, but he will respond:

– I am not in a position to intercede, but you should go to Moses! He is the one who has spoken with Allah…

When they come to Moses (peace be upon him) and express to him their need for intercession, he will in turn tell them:

– I am not in a position to intercede! You should go to Jesus (peace be upon him). He is called the Word and the Soul of Allah…

They will finally make their way to Jesus (peace be upon him), but he will tell them:

– I am not in a position to intercede! You should go to Muhammad (peace be upon him).

They ultimately will then come to me and I will say:

– Yes, this privilege has been given to me.

Then I will request permission to go before my Lord. This permission will be granted. At that moment, some words of praise, which I do not know now, will be revealed to me. I will praise my Lord with these words and will prostrate before him. At that moment, Allah will say to me:

– O Muhammad! Raise your head! Speak! Your speech will be heard. Ask! Your wishes will be fulfilled! Intercede! Your intercession will be accepted.

Then I will say,

– O my Lord! I request for my Community, I request for my Community!

Allah, the Most High, will say,

– O Muhammad! Walk and bring out those whose faith is as light as a grain of barley.

I will do as I have been told. Then, I will return back and will repeat the same words of praise and afterwards will prostrate. Again, I will be told.

– O Muhammad! Raise your head! Speak! Your speech will be heard. Ask! Your wishes will be fulfilled! Intercede! Your intercession will be accepted.

Again, I will say,

– O my Lord! I seek for my Community! I seek for my Community!

Allah will say:

– Walk and bring out those whose faith is as light as an atom or as a mustard seed!

I will go and will do as I have been told. Thereafter, I will return again. Using the same words of praise, I will praise my Lord and will prostrate. Allah will tell me:

– O Muhammad! Raise you head! Speak! Your speech will be heard. Ask! Your wishes will be fulfilled! Intercede! Your intercession will be accepted.

I will say,

– O my Lord! I petition for my community! I petition for my community!

Allah, the Most High, will say,

– Walk and bring out those whose faith is much, much lighter, lighter even than a mustard seed!

I will proceed to do as I have been told and will come back for the fourth time. I will praise Allah with the same words of praise and will prostrate once again.

Allah, the Most High will say,

– O Muhammad! Raise your head! Speak! Your speech will be heard. Ask! Your wishes will be fulfilled! Intercede! Your intercession will be accepted.

This time, I will say:

– O my Lord! Grant me my wish for every one who has said "La ilaha illallah," that is "there is no god but God!"

Allah, the Most High says:

– By My Power, Glory, Highness and Majesty! I will surely bring out those who have said "La ilaha illallah!" [3]

Attaining to these blessings requires staying away from passions and from animal desires through the internalization of the example of Prophet Muhammad, (peace be upon him).

It is related that there was a man who was a Muslim but he did not adopt the example of the Prophet (peace be upon him). One day he saw the Prophet (peace be upon him) in his dream, yet the Prophet (peace be upon him)

---

(3) Bukhârî, *Tawhîd* 36; Muslim, *Îmân* 322; Tirmidhî, *Qıyâmah* 11.

demonstrated no affection towards him. The man became upset and asked:

– "O, Messenger of Allah! Are you unhappy with me?"

– "No!" he replied.

– "But why don't you show me any interest?"

– "Because I do not know you!"

– "How is this possible, Messenger of Allah? I am one of your community. I have heard from scholars that you recognize every one from your community as a mother recognizes her child."

– "Yes, this is true. However, I do not see any signs on you from my example (i.e. sunnah). Besides, no praise (i.e. salawat) has reached me from you. You should know that I recognize one from my Ummah to the extent that he adopts my sunnah."

The man woke up with great sorrow and repented for his sins. He adopted the sunnah of the Prophet (peace be upon him), in his life and sent praises to the soul of the Prophet (peace be upon him). One night, he saw the Prophet (peace be upon him) in his dream again. The Prophet (peace be upon him) said to him:

– "I now recognize you and I will intercede for you."

The Prophet (peace be upon him), had an exceptional nature, worthy of love in all its dimensions. He is the most virtuous and most beautiful being ever to have lived. He is the most compassionate of those who have cried for humanity. He is the only true guide and only true teacher. He is the one who has transformed into loving and compassionate people those whose hearts were so hardened that they were able to bury their daughters alive. He has taught them a holy book and has given them wisdom. To hold him above all else and to love him with boundless passion are signs of the perfection of faith. The apex of such love is illustrated in the following hadith: "No one among you will have perfect faith until he loves me more than his parents, more than his children and more than any other human" [4].

This hadith is an excellent warning and a reminder that one can attain perfection in faith only through total love for the Prophet. The doors of spiritual progress and enlightenment are closed to those who are removed from love of the Prophet. The seed of divine love can grow only in a soil fertile with his love. He is the spring of divine blessings that nurtures the hearts. A heart which loves him compared to a hearts which does not, is like a piece of gold among crude stones.

The moon which reflects light from the sun is a sign of the existence of the sun. In the same way, those saints who have been illuminated with the light of Prophet Muhammad (peace be upon him) are witnesses for him. For this reason whoever says the following words with love in his heart feels a divine spark in his soul:

Ashhadu an la ilaha illallah,

Wa ashhadu anna Muhammadan Abduhu wa Rasuluhu.

---

(4) Bukhârî, Îmân 8; Muslim, Îmân 70; Nasâî, Îmân 19.

That is to say: I bear witness that there is no god but God and I bear witness that Muhammad is his servant and messenger.

Sometimes spiritual passion becomes so overwhelming that the soul feels the pleasure of the indescribable taste of faith. The story of the Bilal of Abyssinia (may Allah be pleased with him), is full of lessons.

Bilal was lonely because he had no one to support him; he had no friend to share in his sorrow. He was a simple slave. Yet, one day he was honored with faith. Afterwards, his faith and his struggle to protect his faith became an outstanding example for the future generations of believers.

He met the Prophet (peace be upon him) and entered the garden of his love. It was as if, with his entire existence he had become part of the Prophet. But his owner who was far removed from the divine light of guidance tied him down on fiery sand and tortured him. His owner mercilessly whipped his naked body. His skin bled. The ignorant crowd around him screamed,

– "You dirty slave! Come back to our way and save yourself!"

Yet, Bilal roared like a wounded lion in the sea of the fiery sand and proclaimed over and over again with all his power "God is one, God is one "

This increased the anger of the uncontrollable crowd and they began beating him more and more... This was not enough to calm them down. So, they tied his neck with a rope and pulled his body around. Against all this, Bilal sought refuge in the love of the Prophet. It was as if he did not feel what was happening to him, as his heart was flooded with the love of Allah and His Messenger. His heart was so happy. Yet, in the physical world he was in a painful situation. He did not even have a hut of his own to sleep in.

Thus, Bilal's love for the Prophet elevated him from slavery to the station of a sultan in the hearts of the believers. He became the muaddhin (i.e. the caller to prayer) of the Prophet and called people to prayer five times a day. He loved the Prophet so much that in his last breath he was saying;

– "Be happy! Be happy! I am returning to the Prophet!" [5]

These were his last words before he departed to the other world.

Therefore, as the hadith that states "one is with the ones he loves" [6], our principle of action on the path to eternity is to follow the Qur'anic verse below:

"So take what the Messenger assigns to you, and deny yourselves that which he withholds from you. And fear Allah; for Allah is strict in Punishment. " (Qur'an, Hashr, 59/7).

O Allah! Please make this humble work so limited in its eloquence a cause for your mercy and your forgiveness and bless us with the truth your Messenger Muhammad has conveyed to humanity. Bless us with the love of your last Messenger. Bless us with his intercession.

✿

---

(5) Ibn Abdilbarr, *al-Istî'âb*, I, 178.

(6) Bukhârî, *Adab* 96; Muslim, *Birr* 165; Tirmidhî, *Zuhd* 50; Dârimi, *Riqaq* 71; Ahmad ibn Hanbal, *al-Musnad*, IV, 395; Ibn Hibbân, *al-Sahîh*, II, 316; al-Humaydî, *al-Musnad*, II, 389

We are aware that our limited words of description, about this personality who represents the zenith of what it means to be a human, are without doubt far away from conveying the fullness of his being. We even feel embarrassed to claim we have introduced him. Our words represent only our powerlessness before such a vast task. What we have humbly aimed for is nothing other than the honor of having made such an intention and of having made such an attempt. He is an infinite world which can be penetrated only to the extent of one's love and one's sincerity towards him.

May Allah bless us by opening our wings in the skies of this spiritual world.

Amin.

BIBLIOGRAPHY

Abû Dâwûd, Sulaymân ibn Ash'ath al-Sijistânî, *al-Sunan*, Istanbul 1413/1992, vol. IV.

Abû Nu'aym al-Isbahâni, Ahmad ibn Abdillah, *Hilyah al-Awliyâ*, Dâr al-Kitâb al-Arabî, Beirut 1405, vol. X.

Abû Ya'lâ, Ahmad ibn 'Ali ibn al-Muthannâ al-Mawsilî al-Tamîmî, *al-Musnad*, ed. Husayn Salîm Asad, Dâr al-Ma'mûn li al-Turath, Damascus, 1404/1984, vol. XIII.

Ahmad ibn Hanbal al-Shaybânî, *al-Musnad*, Istanbul, 1413/1992.

Ahmad ibn Hanbal al-Shaybânî, *Kitâb al-Zuhd*, ed. Dr. Muhammad Jalâl Sharaf, Dâr al-Fikr al-Jâmi'î, Cairo, 1984.

Ahmad ibn Hanbal, *al-Musnad*, Muassasah Qurtubah, Egypt, vol. VI.

Asyalı, Arif Nihat, *Dualar ve Aminler*, Istanbul, 1973

al-Bayhaqî, Abû Bakr Muhammad ibn al-Husayn ibn 'Ali ibn Moses, *al-Sunan al-Kubrâ*, ed.Muhammad 'Abdulkâdir 'Atâ, Maktabah Dâr al-Bâz, Mecca al-Mukarramah 1414/1994, vol. X.

al-Bayhaqî, Abû Bakr Muhammad ibn al-Husayn ibn 'Ali ibn Moses, *Kitâb al-Zuhd al-Kabîr*, ed.al-Shaykh 'Âmir Ahmad Haydar, Muassasah al-Kutub al-Thaqâfiyyah, Beirut, 1996.

al-Bayhaqî, Abû Bakr Muhammad ibn al-Husayn, *Shu'ab al-Îmân*, ed.Muhammad al-Saîd Basyûnî Zaglûl, Dâr al-Kutub al-Ilmiyyah, Beirut 1410, vol. VIII.

al-Bazzâr, Abû Bakr Ahmad ibn 'Amr ibn Abdilhâlık, *Musnad al-Bazzâr*, ed. Dr. MahfuzurRahmân Zaynullah, Muassasah Ulûm al-Qoran & Maktabah al-Ulûm wa'l-Hikam, Beirut-al-Madînah 1409, vol. X.

al-Bukhârî, Abû Abdillah Muhammad ibn Ibrahîm ibn Ismâ'îl al-Ju'fî, *al-Târîkh al-Sagîr*, ed. Mahmûd Abraham Zâyed, Dâr al-Wa'y & Maktabah Dâr al-Turath, Aleppo-Cairo,1397/1977, vol. II.

al-Bukhârî, Abû Abdillah Muhammad ibn Ibrahîm ibn Ismâ'îl al-Ju'fî, *Sahîh al-Bukhârî*, Istanbul 1413/1992, vol.III.

Can Şefik, *Mesnevi Tercemesi*, (Istanbul, 1997).

al-Daylamî, Abû Shujâ' Shîrawayh ibn Shardâr al-Hamazânî, *al-Firdaws bi Ma'sûr al-Khitâb*, ed. El-Saîd ibn Basyûnî Zaglûl, Dâr al-Kutub al-Ilmiyyah, Beirut 1986, vol. V.

al-Dârakutnî, Abû al-Hasan 'Ali ibn 'Umar al-Bagdâdî, *al-Sunan*, ed. al-Sayyid 'Abdullah Hâshim Yamânî al-Adanî, Dâr al-Ma'rifah, Beirut 1386/1966, vol. IV.

al-Dârimî, Abû Muhammad Abdullah, *al-Sunan*, Istanbul 1413/1992.

Ghazali, Abû Hâmid, *al-Munqiz min al-Dalâl*, (Beirut, 1988).

al-Harawî, Abû Ismâîl 'Abdullah ibn Muhammed ibn 'Ali, *al-Arba'în fî Dalâil al-Tawhîd*, ed.Ali ibn Muhammad al-Faqîhî, al-Madînah al-Munawwarah 1404.

al-Hatîb al-Bagdâdî, Abû Bakr Ahmad ibn 'Ali, *Muwaddıh Awhâm al-Jam' va al-Tafrîq*, ed. 'Abdulmu'tî Amîn al-Kal'ajî, Dâr al-Ma'rifah, Beirut 1407, vol.II.

al-Hatîb al-Bagdâdî, Abû Bakr Ahmad ibn 'Ali, *Târikhu Bagdâd*, Dâr al-Kutub al-'Ilmiyyah, Beirut, vol.XIV.

al-Haythamî, 'Ali ibn Abî Bakr, *Majma' al-Zawâid wa Manba' al-Fawâid*, Dâr al-Rayyân li al-Turath-Dâr al-Kitâb al-'Arabî, Cairo-Beirut 1407, vol. X.

al-Hâkim, Abû Abdillah Muhammad ibn Abdillah al-Naysâbûrî, *al-Mustadrak alâ al-Sahîhayn*, ed. Mustafa Abulkâdir 'Atâ, Dâr al-Kutub al-'Ilmiyyah, Beirut 1411/1990, vol. IV.

al-Humaydî, Abû Bakr 'Abdullah ibn al-Zubayr, *Musnad el-Humaydî*, (ed. HabîburRahmân al-A'zâmî), Dâr al-Kutub al-Ilmiyyah & Maktabah al-Mutanabbî, Beirut-Cairo, vol. II.

al-Khourasânî, Abû 'Uthmân Saîd ibn Mansûr, *Kitâb al-Sunan*, (ed. HabiburRahmân al-A'zâmî), al-Dâr al-Salafiyyah, al-Hind (India) 1982.

al-Kissî, Abû Muhammad 'Abd ibn Humayd ibn Nasr, al-*Musnad*, (ed. Subhî Badrî al-Sâmarrâî & Mahmûd Halîl al-Saîdî), *Maktabah al-Sunnah, Cairo 1408/1988.*

al-Marwazî, Abû 'Abdillah Muhammad ibn Nasr ibn al-Hajjâj, *al-Sunnah*, ed. Sâlim Ahmad al-Salafî, Muassasah al-Kutub al-Thaqâfiyyah, Beirut 1408.

185

al-Marwazî, Abû 'Abdillah Muhammad ibn Nasr ibn al-Hajjâj, *Ta'zîm Qadr al-Salât*, (ed.'AbdurRahmân 'Abduljabbâr al-Farîwâî), Maktabah al-Dâr, al-Madînah al-Munawwarah 1406, vol. II.

al-Nabhânî, Yûsuf ibn Ismâ'îl, *al-Anwâr al-Muhammadiyyah min al-Mawâhib al-Ladunniyyah*, Dâr al-Îmân, Damascus 1405/1985.

al-Nasâî, Abû AbdirRahmân Ahmad ibn Shu'ayb, *al-Sunan (al-Mujtabâ)*, Istanbul 1413/1992, vol.III.

al-Nasâî, Abû AbdirRahmân Ahmad ibn Shu'ayb, *al-Sunan al-Kubrâ*, ed. AbdurRahmân Suleiman al-Bundârî, Dâr al-Kutub al-Ilmiyyah, Beirut 1411/ 1991, vol. VI.

al-Qudâ'î, Abû Abdillah Muhammad ibn Salâmah ibn Ja'far, *Musnad al-Shihâb*, ed. Hamdî ibn Abdilmajîd al-Salafî, Muassasah al-Risâlah, Beirut 1407/1986, vol.II.

al-Qurashî, Abû Bakr 'Abdullah ibn Muhammad, *Makârim al-Akhlâq*, ed. Majdî al-Sayyid Ibrahîm, Maktabah al-Qoran, Cairo 1411/1990.

al-Qurtubî, Abû Abdillah Muhammad ibn Ahmad, *al-Jâmi' li Ahkâm al-Qur'ân*, ed. Ahmad 'Abdulalîm al-Barounî, Cairo, Dâr al-Sha'ab 1372, vol. XX.

al-Rabî ibn Habîb ibn 'Umar al-Azdî al-Basrî, *Musnad al-Rabî'*, ed. Muhammad Idrîs & 'Ashûr ibn Yousuf, Dâr al-Hikmah & Maktabah al-Istiqâmah, Beirut-Saltanah 'Ammân 1415.

al-San'ânî, Abû Bakr 'Abdurrazzâk ibn Hammâm, *Kitâb al-Mosannaf*, ed. Habîburranman al-A'zamî, al-Maktab al-Islâmî, Beirut 1403, vol. XI.

al-Shâshî, Abû Saîd al-Haytham ibn Kulayb al-Shâshî, *Musnad al-Shâshî*, ed. Dr. MahfuzurRahmân Zaynullah, Maktabah al-Ulûm wa'l-Hikam, al-Madînah al-Munawwarah 1410, vol. II.

al-Suyûtî, Jalâluddîn 'AbdurRahmân, *Târîkh al-Khulafâ*, ed. Qâsım al-Shimâ'î & Muhammad al-'Uthmânî, Dâr al-Kalam, Beirut 1406/1986.

al-Tabarânî, Abû al-Kâsım Sulaymân ibn Ahmad, *al-Mu'jam al-Awsat*, ed. Târık ibn 'Avadullah & Abdulmuhsin ibn Abraham al-Husaynî, Dâr al-Harâmayn, Cario 1415, vol. X.

al-Tabarânî, Abû al-Kâsım Sulaymân ibn Ahmad, *al-Mu'jam al-Kabîr*, ed. Hamdî ibn 'Abdilmajîd al-Salafî, Maktabah al-'Ulûm va al-Hikam, al-Mawsıl 1404/1983, vol. XX.

al-Tahâwî, Abû Ja'far Ahmad ibn Muhammad bi Salamah, *Sharh Ma'ânî al-Âthâr*, ed. Muhammad Zuhrî al-Najjâr, Dâr al-Kutub al-Ilmiyyah, Beirut 1399, vol. IV.

al-Tayâlisî, Abû Dâwûd Suleiman ibn al-Jârûd al-Basrî, *al-Musnad*, Dâr al-Ma'rifah, Beirut.

al-Tirmidhî, Abû Îsâ Muhammad ibn Îsâ, *al-Sunan*, Istanbul 1413/1992, vol. III.

al-Zahabî, Abû Abdillah Muhammad ibn Ahmad ibn 'Uthmân, *Siyar A'lâm al-Nubalâ*, ed. Shu'ayb al-Arnaût, Muassasah al-Risalah, Beirut 1413, vol. XXIII.

Hannâd ibn al-Sariy al-Kûfi, *al-Zuhd*, ed. 'AbdurRahmân 'Abduljabbâr al-Farîwâî, Dâr al-Hulafâ li al-Kitâb al-Islâmî, al-Kuwait 1406, vol. II.

Ibn 'Abdilbarr, Abû 'Umar Yûsuf ibn 'Abdillah al-Namarî, *al-Istî'âb fî Ma'rifah al-Ashâb*, ed. 'Ali Muhammad al-Bajâwî, Dâr al-Jîl, Beirut 1412, vol.IV.

Ibn 'Abdilbarr, Abû 'Umar Yûsuf ibn 'Abdillah al-Namarî, *al-Tamhîd*, ed. Mustafa ibn Ahmad al-'Alawî & Muhammad 'Abdulkabîr al-Bakrî, Vezarah 'Umûm al-Awqâf, al-Magrib 1387, vol.XXIV.

Ibn 'Adî, Abû Ahmad 'Abdullah ibn 'Adî ibn Muhammad al-Jurjânî, *al-Kâmil fi Du'afâ al-Rijâl*, ed. Yahyâ Muhtâr Gazâvî, Dâr al-Fikr, Beirut 1409/ 1988, vol. VII.

Ibn Abî 'Âsım, 'Amr al-Dahhâk al-Shaybânî, *Kitâb al-Zuhd*, ed. 'Abdulalî 'Abdulhamîd Hâmid, Dâr al-Rayyân li al-Turath, Cairo 1408I.

Ibn Abî Âsım, 'Amr al-Dahhâk al-Shaybânî, *al-Sunnah*, ed. Muhammad Nâsıruddîn al-Albânî, al-Maktab al-Islâmî, Beirut 1400, vol. II.

Ibn Abî Shaybah, Abû Bakr 'Abdullah ibn Muhammad ibn Abî Shaybah al-Kûfî, *al-Musannaf*, (ed. Kamâl Yousuf al-Hût), Maktabah al-Rushd, al-Riyâd 1409, vol. VII.

Ibn al-Jawzî, Abu al-Faraj AbdurRahmân ibn 'Ali ibn Muhammad, *Safwah al-Safwah*, ed. Mahmud Fâkhûrî & Muhammad Rawwâs Qal'ajî, Dâr al-Ma'rifah, Beirut 1399/1979, vol.IV.

Ibn al-Kathîr, Abu al-Fidâ Ismâîl ibn 'Umar al-Qurashî al-Hâfız, *al-Bidâyah wa'n-Nihâyah*, ed. Fuâd al-Sayyid & 'Ali 'Abdussâtir, Dâr al-Kutub al-'Ilmiyyah, Beirut 1408/1988, vol.VIII.

Ibn al-Mubârak, Abû 'Abdillah Abdullah ibn al-Mubârak ibn

Wâdıh al-Marwazî, *al-Zuhd*, ed. HabiburRahmân al-A'zamî, Dâr al-Kutub al-Ilmiyyah, Beirut.

Ibn Hagar al-'Asqalânî, Abu al-Fadl Ahmad, *al-Isâbah fî Tamyîz al-Sahâbah*, (ed. 'Ali Muhammad al-Bajâwî, Dâr al-Jîl), Beirut 1412/1992, wol VIII.

Ibn Hagar al-'Asqalânî, Abu al-Fadl Ahmad, *Fath al-Bârî Sharh Sahîh al-Bukhârî*, ed. Muhammad Fuâd 'AbdulBâqî, Dâr al-Ma'rifah, Beirut 1379, vol. XIII.

Ibn Hagar al-'Asqalânî, Abu al-Fadl Ahmad, *Lisân al-Mîzân*, ed. Dâriah al-Ma'rif al-Nizâmiyyah-India, Muassasah al-A'lamî li al-Matbû'ât, Beirut 1406/1986, vol. VII.

Ibn Hibbân, Abû Hâtim Muhammad ibn Hibbân ibn Ahmad al-Bustî, *al-Majrûhîn*, ed. Mahmûd Abraham Zâyed, Dâr al-Wa'y, Aleppo, vol.III.

Ibn Hibbân, Abû Hâtim Muhammad ibn Hibbân ibn Ahmad al-Bustî, *al-Sahîh*, ed. Shu'ayb al-Arnaût, Muassasah al-Risâlah, Beirut 1414/1993, vol. XVIII.

Ibn Hishâm, *al-Sîrah al-Nabawiyyah*, ed. Mustafa al-Saqqâ & Abraham al-Abyârî, Dâr Ibn Kathîr.

Ibn Ishâq, Muhammad ibn Yasâr, *al-Sîrah (Kitâb al-Mubtada' wa'l-Mab'ath wa'l-Magâzî)*, ed. Muhammad Hamîdullah, Hayra Hizmet Vakfı, Konya 1401/1981.

Ibn Khuzaymah, Abû Bakr Muhammad ibn Ishâq al-Sulamî, *al-Sahîh*, ed.Muhammad Mustafa al-A'zamî, al-Maktab al-Islâmî, Beirut 1390/1970, vol. IV.

Ibn Mâjah, Abû Abdillah Muhammad ibn Yazîd al-Qazwînî, *al-Sunan*, Istanbul 1413/1992, vol. II.

Ibn Sa'd, Abû Abdillah Muhammad ibn Sa'd ibn Manî' al-

Basrî, *al-Tabaqât al-Kubrâ*, Dâr Sâdır, Beirut, vol. VIII.

Imâm Mâlik, Abû Abdillah Malik ibn Anas al-Himyarî, *al-Muwatta'*, Istanbul 1413/1992.

Ma'mar ibn Râshid al-Azdî, *al-Jâmi'*, ed. Habîb al-A'zamî, al-Maktab al-Islâmî, Beirut 1403, vol. II (Published as a part of al-Musannaf of al-San'ânî).

Muslim, Abu'l-Husayn Muslim ibn Hajjâj, *Sahîhu Muslim*, Istanbul 1413/1992, vol. III.

Rûmî, Jalâladdin, *Mathnawî Ma'nawî*, (Tehran, 1378).